HOW TO LEAD AN EXCITING SINGLES MINISTRY

...AND KEEP  IT GOING

DON DAVIDSON

THOMAS NELSON PUBLISHERS
NASHVILLE

Dedication

This book is dedicated to all those singles leaders who want to build exciting and effective ministries for their single adults. Their task is not an easy one. In fact, it is probably the hardest of all the specialized ministries.

They work with a very diverse group of people of all ages, many of whom need the TLC of the church. The need for more "how-to" resources for these ministers has pushed me to create this book. It is my hope and prayer that this material will stimulate these leaders to create exciting programs for their singles.

Published in Nashville, Tennessee, by Thomas Nelson, Inc., and distributed in Canada by Lawson Falle, Ltd., Cambridge, Ontario.

Scripture quotations are from THE HOLY BIBLE, NEW INTERNATIONAL VERSION. Copyright © 1973, 1978, 1984 by the International Bible Society. Used by permission of Zondervan Publishing House. All rights reserved.

Library of Congress Cataloging-in-Publication Data
   How to build an exciting singles ministry—and keep it going / Don Davidson.
     p. cm.
     Includes bibliographical references.
     ISBN 0-8407-4558-3 (pb)
     1. Church work with single people. I. Title.
BV639.S5D38 1993   92-33730
259'.08'852—dc20   CIP

Printed in the United States of America
1 2 3 4 5 6 7 - 97 96 95 94 93

CONTENTS

ACKNOWLEDGMENTS

▲

As a pastor, I had no formal training in the field of single adult ministry. In fact, it was only after my own divorce that I knew such a ministry existed. Hence, much of my training in this field was "on the job."

I wish to thank the various churches where I have served in the area of singles ministry. They graciously allowed me to experiment and learn. Without their support, none of our programs would have been successful.

Thanks also to those singles who participated in our programs and activities. Their support affirmed me in doing what God wanted me to do: serve in the area of single adult ministry.

I would also like to thank all those who have subscribed to my leadership newsletter (Single Adult Ministry Information) and attended my leadership seminars on single adult ministry. Their positive response to my writings and seminars have encouraged me to expand upon that material and put it into book form for a wider audience.

Finally, I would like to thank the editors and staff at Thomas Nelson Publishers for their invaluable help in polishing my manuscript to make it worthy of our audience and God's glory.

PREFACE

For years I have thought about writing a book that would provide various practical insights on doing single adult ministry. It is packed with ideas and step-by-step help for creating an exciting and effective singles ministry.

The material here comes from my seminars on single adult ministry, my own experiences as a singles minister, and from my writings in S.A.M.I. (Single Adult Ministry Information, formerly Single i) a national newsletter for singles leaders, which I have edited since July 1978.

I welcome additional thoughts and ideas regarding single adult ministry. You may send them to me at the Institute of Singles Dynamics, P. O. Box 11394, Kansas City, MO 64112.

My prayer is that the ideas in this book will enable you and your church to minister effectively to the single adults and their families in your congregation and community.

INTRODUCTION

▲

The Single Adult Ministry Phenomenon

Single adults are defined as those who have never married or are divorced or widowed. This group now constitutes the largest minority in the United States numbering some 70 million single adults. This computes to about 40 percent of the adult population and could reach 50 percent by the end of the decade. A group so large simply cannot be ignored!

It seems as if, almost unconsciously, each new decade brings about a new ministry emphasis. The decade of the '50s emphasized the youth ministry aided by the spread of Youth for Christ clubs across the country; the '60s brought the campus movement to our attention with the rise of Campus Crusade for Christ; the emphasis in the '70s was on senior citizen programs; and the '80s has seen a marked acceptance of singles ministry.

Though some churches have had active singles programs for decades, it wasn't until recently that many churches realized the value of developing specialized programs for their single adults. A few denominations now have singles specialists who develop materials, plan conferences, and assist the local church in developing ministries to meet the needs of single people. And a growing number of local churches have expanded their staffs to include ministers to single adults.

Other evidence of growing singles ministries in the United States includes the increasing number of special events planned for singles across the country: seminars, retreats, camps, and conferences. Some denominations sponsor annual "Singles Sundays"and many local churches have a special Sunday when they recognize their single adults. For example, the Baptist Sunday School Board of the Southern Baptist Convention stated that 20.9 percent of the pastors and 41.4 percent of the ministers of education had conducted a seminar, workshop or class on topics of interest to singles within the past twelve months. This denomination also has a national monthly singles magazine, The Christian Single, which has a paid circulation of more than 100,000 copies.[1]

Fortunately, countless churches have started single adult Sunday school classes and many others have opened their doors to some type of a weekly or regular fellowship for singles. Even some rural churches have begun to develop programs for the singles in their area.

While single adult ministry is gaining popularity, we are still in the early stages of this highly specialized work. There is still much to do—there is a need for more books, more curriculum, more Sunday school classes, a better understanding of single adults, and a greater emphasis on the needs of singles in churches throughout the country.

HOW TO USE THIS BOOK

The purpose of this book is to help your church start a singles group. It also provides practical information on how to manage the group, as well as many ideas to help grow an exciting and successful ministry.

Part One explores general issues involved in planning and beginning a single adult ministry in your church. Topics include assessing the need for single adult ministry in churches; the single adult leader; electing officers and instituting committees; and establishing a good planning process.

Part Two offers a more detailed look at the various facets of single adult ministry such as the single adult Sunday school class; support groups, activities, and service projects. Each chapter is packed with practical tips and suggestions for successful single adult programs.

A variety of forms and sample materials appear throughout the book to help plan and manage a successful singles group. You may duplicate and adapt or modify any of these forms to suit the needs of the single adult ministry in your church.

Working with single adults is an enjoyable, rewarding ministry. As you consider beginning a single adult ministry in your church, remember to have fun—share the joy of life in Christ with some very special, wonderful people.

PART ONE

▲

Getting Started

▲

Single Adult Ministry and the Local Church

Ministry among adult singles is one of the greatest mission fields in America today. Single-parent families constitute about 25 percent of all families and represent the fastest growing type of household in the United States. The single adult population is approximately 37 percent of the total adult population, or 65 million singles.[1] Only 15 percent of them go to church, which means that there are some 55 million unchurched single adults in this country alone.

Lyle Schaller, nationally known church growth expert, suggests that if a church wants a new mission field, it should reach out to single persons and single-parent families in its community.[2] Every church has single adults, and there is a need in every church for a ministry to single adults. If your church wants to grow, a natural place to start is with the singles attending your church, then you can bring the ministry to unchurched singles in your community.

WHO ARE YOUR SINGLES?

A ministry to single adults includes working with

never-married, divorced, and widowed persons. If your church is located near a university, your single adult ministry may have a large number of young never-marrieds in attendance. Many of them may not consider themselves singles; instead they would think of themselves as being college age or post-college, but not necessarily single. However, many college singles are attracted to thriving programs labeled College and Career Singles.

Divorced people easily account for the majority of singles in most congregations. Some churches take a hard stand against divorce. But the fact remains that many thousands of people divorce each year. It is estimated that the divorce rate among churchgoers is somewhere between 20 and 30 percent. This means that there are a lot of hurting people in our congregations, people who need to be loved and cared for instead of ignored and alienated. Our congregations are punctuated with persons who carry varying degrees of guilt over their divorce. One of the most redemptive ways your church can care for divorced persons is to let them know that the church understands the reality of divorce and that divorced persons are still valued members of the congregation.

Some years ago, I came across the following response from a single woman who wrote of her own frustration over the narrow view some churches have on divorce. She wrote,

Just because I married the wrong man for all the wrong reasons, does that mean that we should have stayed together to make it right? We prayed four years for our feelings to change and for our marriage to change. We saw counselors and went to Marriage Encounter groups. Still we found that we disliked each other more and more. Rather than continue to tear each other down, after five years of marriage we decided to get a divorce. It was the lesser of two evils—either decision we made would have been painful. . . . Divorce shouldn't be a panacea, but preventative medicine to keep two people from destroying one another.

Here is a testimony of another single-again person who was helped by a church-sponsored singles group. This testimony typifies tens of thousands of single people (many previously unchurched) who have been helped by church singles groups across the country.

I recovered through church. I joined a group of church singles and found out how the other half lives. I used to think that most organized religion was too phony, too rigid. I now recommend that super-critical divorced persons find a church that believes in living what they preach—they will find their lives changed. I had heard that if you were divorced, you weren't welcome in church. But there are quite a few single men and women in our group who are divorced. It's not something that's held over your head. I have read the Bible and I know that it mentions being forgiven more than it mentions being judged. . . . There's a reason.

It is important for your church to make the effort to reach out to these often-ignored people.

Most churches are more comfortable with widowed people in the congregation. Widowers will make a valuable contribution to singles ministry in your church. Their experience of profound loss of loved ones often makes them wise, empathetic counselors and ministers to hurting people in your congregation.

Regardless of age or stage (divorced, never-married,

or widowed), all single persons benefit from spiritual nurture, good fellowship, and a variety of fun activities provided by your church's single adult ministry.

THE VALUE OF CHURCH SINGLES GROUPS

Singles groups provide a wholesome atmosphere where single adults can enjoy worthwhile Christian programs and activities. Such groups also provide an emotional safety net for single adults who don't know where else to go to rebuild their lives after the loss of a job, the death of a spouse, or a divorce. These groups also provide havens for singles moving into the area; a good singles group becomes their extended family in a new town. Single adult groups offer opportunities for personal growth and active involvement in leadership positions.

For many people, single adult ministries are a lifeline offering interesting programs, activities, and a lively network of good friends. Singles groups offer opportunities to minister to people within their church and community. Singles who benefit from church programs are very likely to join that church.

Mike Washburn, singles minister at Richland Hills Church of Christ in Fort Worth, said, "I think the singles ministry holds one of the greatest potentials for evangelism today. We don't have to cultivate our prospects—they are already there. They are drawn to our programs out of deep need." And a leader of a major denomination once said that his denomination could reverse declining membership if churches would reach out to the single adults in their community.

Many single adults who become active in the church also become candidates for leadership positions in a variety of other ministries in the church. Some of these people were active in a previous church before their divorce or before they moved away and are glad to minister again in their new church.

Part of the church's mission is reaching out to widows and orphans (see James 1:27), demonstrating love and acceptance to the divorced and brokenhearted, and providing wholesome fellowship opportunities for all singles. More people attending various singles activities translates into more people who have been brought into contact with the meaning and message of the church, as lived out through the lives of Christian single adults.

FACTORS THAT CONTRIBUTE TO A SUCCESSFUL SINGLE ADULT MINISTRY

Several factors contribute to a successful single adult ministry in your church. First, single adults are looking for quality relationships. Many have tried the bar scene and found it lacking. Others confess that they are bored with staying at home and want something better in life. Many single people attend church groups across the country because they view the church as a safe place to meet good people. Though there have been exceptions, the idea is "If you can't trust the people you meet in church, who can you trust?"

A successful single adult ministry will help singles to develop quality relationships. If you plan all activities and programs with this in mind, your group will be more exciting for those who attend.

All people like to be with others who really care about them. Admittedly, these caring friendships can be found in non-church groups. But genuine love and caring abounds in church singles groups. One only needs to visit a few groups of both kinds to experience the difference. This caring bond of friendship is the common denominator that undergirds the vast majority of church-sponsored singles groups. People will return to a group where they feel loved and wanted.

Church singles groups must provide a well-rounded set of activities and programs to meet the needs of their single adults. A balanced program includes: discussion groups, coping seminars, support groups, Bible studies, cultural events, outreach to others, socials, recreational activities, prayer and share times, and activities for the children of the single parents. Groups that provide balanced and varied programming will thrive and survive. Groups that offer only one item on the program menu soon find that their singles get tired of the same old diet. (A later chapter discusses in detail how to offer a balanced program.)

Your group will also draw some single parents. Your church must meet their needs as well. Try to include their children in some of your group's activities. One advantage to this is that the children will have an opportunity to meet their parent's adult friends. It is easier for the children when Mom or Dad go to an adult-only activity because the kids know who their parents are with. And getting the kids involved in some of the group's activities is often the door through which kids enter the church.

A successful single adult ministry also provides spiritual input. It is natural to expect this from any church that takes its mission seriously. Even non-Christians who attend the singles group will expect, or at least tolerate, spiritual emphasis.

You should plan specific teaching and prayer times for the group, but there will be other times when spirituality is not the focus of the meeting. At these social activities, you can still announce religious events and programs in a very low-key manner that will not "run off" those who are not interested in that aspect of your ministry. Another unobtrusive way to offer opportunities for spiritual input is to print religious events in a monthly activities calendar. Either way, all who hear or attend will know what you stand for and that they are invited to share in those spiritual times too.

There should be little or no pressure for outsiders or non-Christians to attend church wide religious programs, but the church must make them available for those single adults who are searching for spiritual guidance. They will discover that this spiritual aspect is really what gives meaning to life. Like anyone else, single persons need the message of hope which the gospel offers.

A critical factor in developing a single adult ministry is the church's providing enough staff time to insure its success. While only a small percentage of churches have full-time professional directors or singles ministers, many other churches assign a staff person, such as an associate minister or the director of Christian education, to oversee the singles program.

The majority of churches who have professional leadership for their singles programs usually succeed. If all the responsibility is placed on lay people to run the program, the ministry often dies because of burnout or "other interests" (often translated as a new romance). Having the professional support and oversight of a staff member directly determines the success of your single adult ministry.

And then there is the matter of money. Churches with successful singles programs make some available to further the cause. If the church really believes in its ministry to single adults, it must budget money each year to help finance the expenses of the program. Putting money behind the singles ministry to insure its success shows the congregation that your church values single people.

Your church can have a dramatic impact for Christ

in the lives of single adults. Before discussing how to begin a single adult ministry in your church, let's look at a variety of ways your church can immediately touch the lives of single people in your congregation.

HOW THE CHURCH CAN AFFIRM AND INVOLVE SINGLES

There are many things your church can do to affirm and support its single members. Here are twenty suggestions to help communicate to singles that they are loved and valued members of the family of God. Read through the list of suggestions and choose those you want to implement in your church.

Once you have recorded your selections, begin to implement them by talking with the pastoral staff and/or board. You may want to recruit two or three other people from the congregation to help you and pray with you as you reach out to the single adults in your church.

1. Cultivate a positive attitude toward singles ministry. Communicate to staff, board members, and the congregation that this work is not an optional program but a vital component of the mission of the whole church.

2. Listen to single people's needs and desires. Really hear what they are saying. What they tell you will shape your church's single adult ministry.

3. Jot down ideas for programs that meet their needs. Your list may include a singles Sunday school class; special support groups; coping seminars; and social and recreational opportunities.

4. Be sensitive to terminology and nomenclature that is demeaning to single adults. For example, avoid naming a singles class Spares and Pairs. Also avoid calling the standard February banquet a Sweetheart Banquet—many singles no longer have a sweetheart to accompany them. Instead call it a Valentine Banquet or a Midwinter Banquet. (See Ch. 13, "Activities," for ideas on special days and holidays). Also, avoid referring to divorced homes as "broken" or "fractured." Such labels hurt everyone living in these families.

5. Encourage your pastor to use positive illustrations about single individuals and single parents in his or her sermons. Negative illustrations (or being completely overlooked) tend to further alienate singles from the church.

6. The pastor can give single adults moral support by affirming their activities from the pulpit.

7. Encourage married members of the congregation to attend an occasional singles activity. This shows that the church pays attention to what singles do and are interested in their programs.

8. Nominate responsible single adults to church boards and committees.

9. Encourage and equip singles to serve in all positions within the church, including the worship service.

10. Include singles activities in the church newslet-

ter and other places where church events are publicized.

11. Stock the church library with representative books dealing with singles concerns and issues. Consult a local Christian bookstore for suggestions of available books.

12 When selling tickets to church events, do not offer discounts for couples. For example, do not price tickets to an ice cream social at $5 for singles and $9 for couples. That shows discrimination against singles and favoritism toward couples.

13. Provide free child care every time there is an official event at the church, including singles events.

14. Provide free counseling for all singles. Some may be wrestling with divorce or post-divorce issues, others may need help with grief or feelings of self-esteem. Whatever the concern, offer to listen.

15. Begin a Family Adoption Program in which church families regularly invite a single or a single-parent family to join them for a meal or family activity.

16. Be sensitive and attentive to the particular needs of single persons during the holiday season. (For suggestions, see Special Days and Holidays in Ch. 12.)

17. Encourage singles to help organize church-spon-

sored social events, such as square dancing, auctions, Christmas caroling, historical tours, etc.

18. Include the concerns of single members in pastoral prayers.

19. Help singles who are new to the church and community connect with other singles quickly. Introduce them to as many individuals in the church as possible, and encourage these new friendships.

20. Offer various types of information workshops and seminars on topics such as: taxes, divorce and grief recovery, single parenting, budgeting, bargain-hunting, etc.

While there are thousands of churches across the country that now offer viable programs for their single adults, some churches still resist the effort to create any special classes, programs, or activities for their single adults. One of the reasons church leaders often give for not developing anything special for singles is that they are no different from anyone else. Some pastors believe that their single adults should attend the regular church programs and don't need anything else.

In the next chapter we will consider how single adults are different from married adults. They have needs that a "married adult" class probably cannot meet. If you are not already convinced of the value of starting a singles ministry, these differences should compel you to rethink your position.

▲

CHAPTER 2

Important Things to Understand About Single Adults

As we prepare to develop our ministry to, with, and for single adults, we ought to know some of the dynamics that affect this group of wonderful but often hurting people. Single adults, as a broad demographic group of people, differ somewhat from the rest of the adult population.

As we enumerate these differences, remember that not all singles have all of these characteristics. The vast majority of single adults are whole and healthy people, and they are quite a diverse group. Nevertheless, at any given time, some single adults in your church will probably have some of these characteristics. And statistically, most singles will have some of these characteristics at some time in their lives.

As a singles leader, your effectiveness in working with single adults will be directly related to how well you understand their differences, their needs, the myths surrounding being single, and their attitudes toward the church.

SOME OF THE DIFFERENCES

Single adults are like other adults in many ways, but as a group, they tend to be different. It is important that you, as a single adult leader, understand these ten basic differences. They will help you to focus some of the activities and support groups you choose to start.

Different Priorities

While some priorities are the same as those of married people (job satisfaction, financial security, good relationships, etc.), other single adults' priorities are unique to them. According to an Institute of Life Insurance survey, four times as many singles as marrieds picked "developing as an individual" as a major life goal. And eleven times as many singles as marrieds listed "a fulfilling career" as their major life goal. Marrieds, on the other hand, picked "a happy family life" as their major aim twice as often as single adults.[1] Even when they desire the same things, how single people try to achieve those goals and how important each goal is will likely be different from their married friends.

Spontaneity

Many singles seem to prefer living moment to moment, instead of making plans in advance. The majority of single adults wait until the last possible moment to make a definite commitment to do something, unless it is something they really want to do. Although this makes planning an event more difficult, single adults have an advantage in being able to accept fun, spur-of-the-moment invitations that marrieds cannot. Married people generally must make plans earlier so their partners can plan accordingly.

Loose Family Ties

According to some researchers at Louisiana State University, singles don't have as many close family ties as do marrieds.[2] The researchers state that unmarried adults (specifically those who are divorced or have never married) not only have fewer ties to kin than married couples, but their social ties in general are "less dense than those of the marrieds." In addition, they have known their fewer friends for shorter periods of time. This lack of networking often results in a weaker support system for times of crisis.

"Church-Hopping"

Single adults often do not have the same level of commitment to a one-church concept as do married couples. According to an article in Ministry Currents, singles are nearly twice as likely as marrieds to attend more than one church.[3] There are a variety of reasons for this. Single adults who do not have young children at home or a spouse's schedule to consider, may find that this is a good time in life to visit around without making a commitment anywhere. They may simply enjoy the variety of experiences. Some singles (particularly divorced) who were once involved in a home church may no longer feel comfortable there, so they float around, looking for a new church they can call home. Or they may attend their home church some, but also attend one that their current "significant other" attends. Or single adults may attend their home church and another church that has a strong singles program.

Limited Resources of Single Parents

When a household divides, the whole family's standard of living often drops. However, the custodial parent's lifestyle (and that of the children) usually suffers the most because he or she must spread limited resources thinner to care for the children. One or both parents may have to scale down expectations or take an extra job to pay the bills. Further, custodial single parents don't have as much time for outside activities as they did when they shared the household duties with a spouse.

Children of Single Parents

In an analysis of a nationwide survey conducted in 1988, researchers for the National Center of Health Statistics found a remarkably high incidence of emotional and academic problems among children living in single-parent families and step families. Childhood learning disabilities occurred in 5.5 percent of mother-father families, 7.5 percent in mother-only families, 9.1 percent in mother-stepfamilies, and 8.3 percent in other family situations. The findings also revealed an even more striking pattern: "Young people from single-parent families or stepfamilies were two to three times more likely to have had emotional problems than those who had both of their biological parents present in the home."[4] Children in any environment may have problems; it doesn't happen only in divorced families. And many, many children of single-parent homes become very successful citizens. However, the overwhelming evidence is that children of single parents are prone to more emotional and academic problems than children living with both of their natural parents.

Loneliness

Everyone desires human companionship. We need someone to listen to us and share our ups and downs. But if a person lives alone, as many single adults do, it takes more time and energy to find someone to listen. Psychologist Jeffrey Young of Philadelphia says,

"People who live alone tend to say that they are lonely more frequently than people living with others."[5] This point is supported by a 1991 study in Arizona. Researchers investigated the prevalence of loneliness among 8,600 adults. They found that 20 percent of divorced and 15 percent of never-married adults reported feeling lonely "fairly often" or "very often" during the year before the survey. These statistics compare to less than 5 percent of married adults who responded.[6]

Giving Up on Life

Living alone or feeling alienated from family or friends can lead to clinical depression, a sense of hopelessness, and sometimes to suicidal thoughts. People in all categories of singleness have a higher suicide rate than married adults, but the most vulnerable are the divorced and separated. Researchers at the Johns Hopkins School of Hygiene and Public Health concluded, "The risk of a suicide attempt was an estimated eleven times greater for the separated or divorced as compared with other marital groups."[7] Even when someone does not have serious suicidal thoughts, he or she still searches for meaning, hope, and a reason to live. Close friendships can help.

Greater Stress

According to the Holmes-Rahe Social Readjustment Rating Scale, there is nothing more traumatic than becoming single again: The top two stress-producers are the death of a spouse and divorce. When either of these occurs, it usually produces other changes, which, in turn, cause even more stress: change of address, a job change, legal battles, change in social networks, decline in lifestyle, financial readjustments, and so forth. Divorced and widowed persons usually experience a huge amount of stress in the first two years following a change in their marital status.

Health Problems

Another result of loneliness is that it poses serious health risks. One research article reports that separated and divorced persons "suffer more chronic and acute illnesses . . . and visit their physicians 30 percent more frequently than do their married or single counterparts." The article continues by saying that they "have significantly greater mortality rates from certain diseases, including pneumonia, tuberculosis, heart disease, and some types of cancer."[8] And finally, medical evidence seems to indicate that the death rate due to heart disease among divorced men is twice the rate for married men.[9]

Depressing, isn't it? While these observations do not describe all single adults, they do describe some who will be in your group. These problems will probably surface more often in your single adult ministry than in any other ministry in your church. As a result, we cannot simply dismiss creating special programs for single adults on the basis that they are exactly the same as everyone else. They aren't. The church can provide the friendship, support, and encouragement that unmarried people especially need. Once we understand their needs, we are well on our way to laying the foundation for an effective and exciting singles ministry.

SOME OF THE SPECIAL NEEDS YOU CAN MEET

All people, regardless of age or marital status, need to feel loved and appreciated. But this is a greater need among many singles as they struggle with feelings of not being chosen or of being rejected as a marriage partner. Ministry leaders should concentrate on building a sense of self-worth in their single adults. They should also look for ways to build long-term relationships and a strong sense of community among the singles in their church. Other special "felt needs" among single adults include career planning, financial guidance, single-parenting advice, time for leisure activities, closer friendships, a chance to start over, significance in other people's lives, and the desire for spiritual growth. Your ministry can offer workshops, field trips, speakers, classes, retreats, and support groups to help singles work through problems or develop their own potential. And your social get-togethers can promote emotional intimacy and make life more enjoyable for single adults. Single adults who attend church expect to have many of their needs met through loving fellowship of the church and its singles ministry. If the church fails to meet these needs, the singles will either move on to another church group or quit going to church altogether.

SOME OF THE MYTHS

Over the years, I have collected many myths about singles. They come from a variety of sources—pastors, lay people, modern society. Have you ever heard something like this:

- Single people sin more.
- All singles are "wild swingers."
- Single adults are just kids who never grew up.
- All singles want to marry.
- Single adults are not complete without marriage partners.
- Single people have all the time in the world.
- Singles always enjoy being and doing things alone.
- Singles have an easy life.

- Single adults have major problems; if they didn't, they would be married.
- If you're single, you're rich and have no bills.
- Getting married solves all the loneliness of single people.
- Singles are irresponsible and undependable.
- Single adults are bad parents.
- Single women cannot make it on their own identity; they must derive their identity and status from a man.
- Single adults don't understand family life.
- All singles are lonely.
- All single men who live together must be gay.
- Single people are a threat to married couples.
- Single adults are only interested in sex and having a good time.
- Single adults are not well-rounded individuals.
- Single people are failures.
- Single men and women are selfish and set in their ways.
- Single parents are less capable of providing a loving home for their children than are two parent families.

These notions are no more true of single adults than of married adults. Most single individuals are intelligent, friendly, successful, spiritual people who happen not to be married. Some single adults do not even want to be married because they are already content with their lives and relationships! They simply struggle with life's issues from a different perspective and with different resources than married people do. The church must begin to accept the truth about single adults—with all the positives and negatives—and help them to grow.

THE ATTITUDE OF THE CHURCH

While single adults have begun to return to the church, historically only about 15 percent of all single people attended church. According to one report, 87 percent of all single adults who used to attend church regularly do not attend now.[10] They don't feel wanted or recognized.

Traditionally, the church has not recognized singles as equal with marrieds. Many churches seemed to have an unwritten rule that an unmarried person could not serve within the church. They could not teach classes, head committees, lead worship, work with children's groups, assist in church administration, lead Bible studies, or start their own support groups. The needs and talents of single people have been virtually ignored.

Many churches have come a long way in accepting the service of single adults. But unfortunately, even today, some still refuse to allow single persons to hold positions of leadership within the church, especially if they are divorced. This sends the signal that single adults in general (and divorced persons in particular) are not good enough to serve, that they are less than whole, and therefore not really wanted in the church. It's almost as if they have a disease and church leaders fear their contaminating others.

Because of specific commands in the Bible, the church is usually more sympathetic to widows and, as a result, most widowed persons stay in church. According to a 1988 Gallup Religion Poll, when a marriage ends in the death of a spouse, the survivor's religious ties often intensify.[11] But when a marriage ends in divorce, the couple's religious involvement often decreases sharply. The report continues by saying that those who are separated or divorced often feel alienated from their church, complaining that the church focuses only on the needs of intact families. If a single person wants to grow spiritually, it would seem the church is not the place to find help.

Another, more subtle, type of rejection comes when

church leaders and staff refuse to recognize that singles are different and refuse to help set up a single adult Sunday school class or support group.

No wonder single adults have not stayed in church!

Today's church must come to grips with the fact that approximately 40 percent of the adult population in America is not married. Many of these people grew up in the church and would like to return. They have many gifts that can enrich our life in the modern church. The question is: Will the church accept them as first-class citizens with full rights of worship and service, or will it continue to ignore and alienate them?

The following anonymous quote sums up the best way for a church to respond to its single members:

> The greatest ministry a church can offer is to love and accept people without judging who they are by age, occupation, race, or marital status. . . . It can provide ministry applicable to all parts of the congregation without encouraging factions.

> The church can work together to provide a ministry to single adults which does not alienate them from the church family. This can only be done as members of the church understand the actual needs of the single population. It is important to erase erroneous concepts that have developed concerning the single adult.

> An understanding of those to whom we minister is . . . vitally important.

CHAPTER **3**

▲

The Single Adult Leader

The single adult leader is the person directly in charge of the singles program and ministry. About two-thirds of the leaders in single adult ministry are paid staff persons. The other one-third of the leaders are lay volunteers.

Most small churches rely on lay leadership, while large churches put staff persons in charge. The medium-sized churches frequently use both laity and staff as leaders in single adult ministry.

A concerned lay person often starts a singles ministry in his or her church. Unfortunately, many programs eventually fail without direct staff involvement. Unless churches assign staff to oversee the ministry, lay leadership often suffers burnout, and the single adult ministry disappears. To paraphrase Proverbs 28:18, "Where there is no staff, the program perishes."

Churches serious about launching and maintaining a singles ministry must assign a staff person to work with that ministry. Generally the more time and energy a staff person has to devote to singles ministry, the greater its chances for growth and success.

THE MARITAL STATUS OF THE LEADER

An important issue in single adult ministry concerns whether the leader should be married or single. Let's examine the advantages and disadvantages of single leaders and married leaders.

The Leader as a Single Person

The primary advantage of a single leader is that singles better understand other singles. Some insist that only single people can lead because they identify with the needs of other singles. Because there are so many divorced people in singles groups, some argue that the singles leader should be a divorced person.

It is often difficult for happily married people to understand the pain and trauma of becoming single again through divorce or the death of one's spouse. It is true that a single-again person can better relate to divorced or widowed singles because they have firsthand experience.

However, there are a couple of disadvantages to single leaders. A single leader's motives may be questionable. Some single leaders have a hidden agenda regarding opposite-sex singles and therefore may not always have the best interest of the group at heart. Even if a single leader's motives are pure and honorable, other singles in the group may become suspicious if they see their leader spending too much time or showing too much attention to a single of the opposite sex. A woman singles leader in her early thirties told me that the women in her group often became suspicious if they saw her talking too long with any man near her age attending the group. They felt jealous because they thought she was fostering a romance with the man. For the sake of group harmony and integrity, most single leaders are

advised to have a standing policy not to become roman-
tically involved with anyone in their group.

There is another seeming disadvantage to single
leaders. Some churches think it's unscriptural to hire
or appoint a single person—especially a divorced person—to any church leadership position. These churches
only hire or appoint married people to leadership positions. They usually base this decision on their interpretation of 1 Timothy 3:2, which says that a person who
aspires to be a church leader should be "the husband of
but one wife."

In my opinion, these churches have not correctly
exegeted 1 Timothy. As I understand it, the Greek
indicates that leaders should be the type who, if married, are married to only one person at a time. The
culture in that day allowed for polygamy, and Paul
wrote to young Timothy to advise against church
leaders' having more than one wife at a time. If single
people were not allowed to serve as leaders, Jesus would
not have been eligible to serve on these church staffs!
Neither would the apostle Paul have been eligible (if you
consider him to have been single, as many scholars do).
This interpretation also would eliminate the work of all
the wonderful single women and men who have served
the church in so many ways through the centuries.

There is also a specific disadvantage to a single
parent as leader. A custodial single parent with young
children at home may not be accessible or flexible in his
or her schedule. Leaders often need to be "on call" for
their group. A single person with no children often is
more accessible to the group and is more available when
needed on the job. However, when a church does hire a
single parent with young children, the singles ministry
and the entire congregation must accept and appreciate
that person's right to days off and time alone with his
or her children.

The Leader as a Married Person

Despite the difference in marital status, there are some advantages to married people serving as singles leaders. Married leaders team up with their spouses to be good role models for singles. When both the husband and wife are active in the singles program, they demonstrate how married people can be loving, caring, and respectful of each other.

Married leaders also have the advantage in counseling situations. To avoid suspicion and jealousy, husbands can counsel with single men and wives counsel single women.

However, a disadvantage to happily married couples working as singles leaders is that they may not be able to understand the trauma and pain of divorce or the death of a spouse. Still, most leaders have experienced issues of loss, grief, or anger in their families or with close friends. A leader who is sensitive to the needs of people often relates quite well to single adults in crisis and does a splendid job directing the overall singles program.

Another significant disadvantage to married people as singles leaders is that, I believe, most happily married couples do not know how difficult it is to be a single parent. I once read a story about an Air Force chaplain who said, "Whenever I feel overwhelmed by the demands of my work and home life, I am humbled by thinking about the responsibilities that a single parent faces daily." The chaplain added that he learned a lot about the responsibilities of single parents by listening to them at chapel. He noted, "Sometimes I am frustrated when I go home from work and remember I still have to mow the yard. I also have to remember my wife is cooking dinner, and she worked all day too. Single parents have to go home, mow the yard, and fix dinner, in addition to getting the children ready for bed."

Married leaders must understand and communicate that they know it is difficult for a single parent to try to do the work of two parents. Leaders must be sensitive to the emotional, physical, and financial stresses single parents suffer. I recommend that married leaders schedule regular meetings with single parents to listen to their feelings and concerns. They need to understand why single parents can't possibly attend all the activities and programs offered by the ministry. It is very difficult for single parents to fulfill all their responsibilities at home and then attend outside functions too. Leaders should express compassion and a willingness to help in these situations.

One way in which married leaders can minister significantly to a single parent is to program activities which include children or to arrange for a baby-sitter at the church. One of the quickest ways to any parent's heart is to care deeply for his or her children. Even the single parents who do not normally attend church services will be attracted to your thoughtful plans.

Married or Single—Which is Best?

In my opinion, the most qualified person for single adult leadership is one who married later in life or, better yet, remarried after a divorce or the death of a spouse. This leader offers the best of both worlds—the leader can identify with singles because he has experienced his own pain and trauma of becoming single again, and as a remarried person he offers the advantages married leaders bring.

But whether single or married, the most important qualification is to be highly sensitive to the issues and needs facing single adults in the church and community. Married people can make outstanding single adult leaders. All they need is a sensitive, loving spirit and a willingness to listen carefully to the needs of those under their care.

CHARACTERISTICS OF A GOOD SINGLE ADULT LEADER

A simple list of characteristics for a good single adult leader is an acrostic of the word leadership. Each letter in the acrostic stands for a particular qualification:

Listener   A good single adult leader is a good listener. Many singles want to tell their story—good listening skills are a must.

Enthusiastic   A good single adult leader is enthusiastic about his or her work and the various programs and activities of the singles ministry. Singles will catch their enthusiasm for the ministry from the leader.

Accepting   A good single adult leader accepts everybody, no questions asked. All too often single people feel rejected and unwanted. The leader must demonstrate an attitude of acceptance. I often say in my leadership seminars that the leader must, figuratively speaking, walk around with his or her arms open and the palms extended upward, a living symbol of acceptance.

Democratic   A good single adult leader helps singles take responsibility for their group. A good leader never pushes singles into doing things they don't want to do. Instead, a good leader helps singles implement activities and programs that meet the needs of the group.

Encouraging   A good single adult leader is an encourager, one who uplifts people and gives hope to the group.

Resourceful   A good single adult leader is resourceful. He or she works to be on the cutting edge of singles ministry by attending leadership seminars; subscribing to appropriate periodicals; reading books on the subject; and learning from other singles ministries.

Sensitive   A good single adult leader must be very sensitive to the problems, needs, and issues facing singles as individuals and as a group.

Happy   A good single adult leader is happy. Unhappy people alienate others; happy people attract them. A leader who is not a happy person will drive people away in spite of other excellent skills.

Inspiring   A good single adult leader leads by inspiration, not manipulation. A good leader is excited about the work and motivates others to catch the vision.

People-oriented   A good single adult leader must have good people skills and be more focused on people than programs. Successful leaders show great concern for their people. They are not afraid to sacrifice policy to help people. Remember, Jesus died for people, not programs. Good leaders put people first!

Good single adult leaders are also good managers. There are three skills good managers use in their work:

- Technical skills—the ability to do the job well.
- Human skills—the ability to work with people and to help them reach their goals.
- Conceptual skills—the ability to see the big picture in planning, organizing, and using resources.

Good singles leaders also use these managerial skills in their ministry. Let's focus on the importance of the last item, conceptual skills.

Conceptual skills enable leaders to understand how one program affects another; how one activity complements another; how a new policy might conflict with an older, existing policy. Good single adult leaders are wise managers, using their conceptual abilities to integrate the singles programs and activities into the life of the entire congregation.

The leader must see the big picture and understand not only inner workings of the singles program but also how the activities of single adults mesh with other plans and goals of the congregation. The leader is a manager who coordinates plans, resources, and facilities with the rest of the staff. A good singles leader (manager) also integrates the singles program into the total ministry of the church. For example, let's say the singles want to have an ice cream social in the church fellowship hall on a Wednesday night. A good singles leader checks with the youth director to see how the ice cream social might affect the slumber party the youth are having that night in the church building. Or she checks with the pastor about his plans for the Wednesday evening prayer service and how that may preclude another activity from being held at the church that evening.

Being a single adult leader is an exciting and challenging ministry, which blends managerial and people skills. While good managerial skills are important, there is no substitute for loving your people. A plaque on my desk reminds me of this daily: If you have a good relationship, performance is almost irrelevant. If you don't, the performance is almost everything.

Quality, caring relationships with and among singles

is the hallmark of good single adult leadership. In other words, good single adult leaders are also good pastors.

PASTORAL CARE OF SINGLE ADULTS

Quality pastoral care of single adults requires following a few general guidelines. All single adult leaders must recognize they are pastoral caregivers. Singles seek out their leaders for counsel, instruction, and a listening ear. Following the guidelines below will enable single adult leaders to become quality pastoral caregivers.

Take the Initiative

Take the initiative to let singles know they are valued and loved. Especially let divorcing couples and divorced individuals in the congregation know they remain important and valuable members of the church. Value and love are expressed through personal letters and visits, as well as through counseling and prayers.

Make a Good First Impression

How you handle people's problems and concerns creates a powerful first impression. Handling singles' problems with care and sensitivity creates a positive first impression. Singles will continue to seek pastoral care from leaders who impress them as wise caregivers.

Single adult leaders must periodically evaluate how they come across to people who seek their help. For example, leaders who spend lots of time helping people may discover they have a tendency to treat all people and their problems in an impersonal manner. Continually check your attitudes and how you treat people. Don't let bad habits creep in.

Remember to make a good impression with someone

who comes to you for the first time seeking help—be available, personal, and concerned.

Teach Biblical Truths

Another task of single adult leaders is to teach. It is important to teach biblical truths, uncovering original meanings as well as making present-day applications. In developing a biblical teaching plan for singles, remember that many single adults have a difficult time coping with life. For example, singles may not want to study Paul's view of eschatology, but they will attend classes dealing with biblical guidelines on coping with pain and getting on with their lives.

In addition to making Bible study relevant to single adults' needs, as a form of pastoral care, leaders must encourage classes and seminars dealing with specific issues.

For example, divorced people must wrestle with the emotional and legal issues surrounding child custody rights. A single adult leader who understands teaching as pastoral care will encourage the planning committee to offer a seminar with a Christian lawyer and psychologist exploring child custody rights.

Remember, quality Bible study and adult education is quality pastoral care.

Be User-Friendly

Pastoral care must be user-friendly. Single newcomers and members alike must easily be able to get the help they seek from the church office, staff, and single adult leaders. Church leaders must communicate to single adults they are available for pastoral care and counsel.

Years ago I had the privilege of working with a woman who was gifted at helping people with their questions. She could often anticipate what you needed even before you asked and always put you at ease when she answered your question. In other words, she was user-friendly. She was eventually promoted to the head of the department, passing over others more academically qualified.

Affirm Your Members

Singles (and everyone else, for that matter) need affirmation. They need to know they are appreciated and accepted.

To borrow an idea from a business newsletter (The Pryor Report), singles leaders can imagine each person in the group wearing a sign around their neck that says, "Please make me feel important!"[1] The sign may be imaginary, but the desire to feel needed, appreciated, and recognized is very real. When leaders praise single adults, they are dispensing quality pastoral care.

A little praise can go a long way toward making singles feel better about themselves and making them feel part of the group. Quality pastoral caregivers affirm God's love for single people and tell them they have a right to build their lives and attend programs and activities.

Be a Good Counselor

Counseling means listening to someone's concerns and, if asked, offering help and advice. Leaders professionally trained in this field can do more, such as administer psychological tests and offer in-depth counseling. But even leaders without professional training can offer pastoral help to single adults.

Individual Counseling.

Single adults often seek out their leader for personal counseling. Sometimes they really want to be counseled and guided. But most often they only want someone to listen to their story. Following a couple of general counseling guidelines improves the quality of pastoral care.

Be professional. Thank the person for seeking your help and promise that the session will be confidential. Let the person tell his story in his own words but let him know in advance the time limits of the session. Stop the session on time, and schedule another session if necessary.

Be cautious. Take necessary precautions to avoid accusations of sexually taking advantage of a counselee. One way to do this is to leave your door ajar or counsel in a room with windows so that your actions can be observed. In addition to taking notes on the session, you might also ask permission to make a confidential tape recording of the conversation. If you suspect your counseling session might be misconstrued, refer the counselee to a same-sex counselor.

Group Counseling

Group counseling may have a trained counselor conduct group counseling sessions or a leader acting as a facilitator who guides the discussion and tries to make sure everyone has a voice. These group sessions are often known as support groups. (See Ch. 12, "Support Groups" for a detailed discussion on this form of counseling.)

Premarital Counseling

Many single adults meet their future mates in singles groups. Single adult leaders who are also ordained ministers are often asked to perform wedding ceremonies and usually offer premarital counseling. However, non-ordained single adult leaders may be asked to offer premarital counseling sessions especially if the couple met in the singles group. As you talk with the couple during these sessions, explain that you just want to talk with them about their thoughts and feelings for each other as they make the transition from single to married life. Check with your local Christian bookstore for books discussing the finer points of premarital counseling. But generally, simply listening to the couples joys and concerns about their new life together is good pastoral care.

Knowing When to Refer

Many single adult leaders who do a lot of pastoral counseling set in advance a maximum number of sessions for working with an individual. There are two reasons for this. It encourages the counselee to get down to the heart of the problem. If you can't help in, say, three visits, the problem is beyond your ability to help and the counselee should seek the services of a professional counselor or therapist.

To help you determine when a referral is appropriate, I have outlined an article by Dick Tibbits about when and how to refer a counselee to a professional.[2]

If you answer yes to any of the following questions, refer the counselee's to a professional immediately.

Intensity of feeling. How much and how deeply is the counselee experiencing grief, anger, jealousy, guilt, loneliness, resentment, or bewilderment? Are these feelings overwhelming him, making it difficult to function normally?

Depth of influence. Is the person's behavior abnormal? Has the counselees problem existed throughout his life-time?

Sense of reality. A psychosis is a clear break with reality in which communication and/or normal ways of relating are not possible. Does the counselee seem completely out of touch with reality?

Behavior. Is the counselee's behavior producing pain or stress for himself or others to the point where the pain is no longer tolerable?

Limitations on your time. Have you exceeded the amount of time you think is appropriate in counseling with this individual?

Limitations to your skill or experience. Are you are no longer able to understand what the counselee is saying and feeling?

Limitations on your influence. Is the counselee too close to you personally for you to offer effective pastoral care? Or does the counselee have influence on your job or function as a leader?

Limitations to your emotional security. Does this person threaten you or make you feel anxious? Or, is the counselee dealing with an issue that you haven't resolved in your own life?

When it is time to make a referral, it should be done very gently so the counselee doesn't feel rejected. Speak of the referral positively. For example, you may say something like, "There is a professional counselor whom I would like you to start seeing. She is very good and I think you two could make progress together. Here's her phone number, name, and address. Would you like to call now to set up your first visit?" Making a referral properly enhances your relationship with the counselee.

As you conclude your final session, tell the counselee you were glad he contacted you in this matter and that you want to be there for him should he ever need your help with other problems or concerns. Invite her to stay in touch with you because you are interested in her progress.

Remember Special Days

Remember single adults on their special days and when they have done something noteworthy. Remembering the important days or special occasions in peoples lives is a genuine form of pastoral care.

Birthdays and Anniversaries

Many single adult leaders send cards at special times to members of the singles group. They often include a short personal note to say that they are glad to have them as members of the group or that they appreciate them and their service to the Lord.

If you don't know birthdays or special anniversaries of the individuals in the singles group, find out and start sending cards next year. Whenever you start it, people will appreciate being remembered and love the personal touch you add!

One of the things my seminary preaching professor said that pastors should do is send first anniversary cards to couples that I united in marriage. Single adult leaders should also remember the first anniversary of singles from their groups who marry. To do this, keep accurate records of couples' addresses and drop them a card to let them know what a joy it was to minister with them in the singles group. If you performed their wedding, mention that too as being one of your special joys of ministry.

Noteworthy Accomplishments

Be aware of the special things single adults do for the ministry and write them a short note to let them know that you are proud of them. Also take notice of any other special accomplishments, achievements, or big promotions.

When bad news strikes, call or send an appropriate card. A simple card or letter acknowledging that you care will be forever prized by many.

CONCLUSION

A successful single adult ministry requires leaders who demonstrate leadership ability; possess fundamental managerial and people skills; and are able to offer sensitive, discerning pastoral care. Single adult leadership is among the most rewarding ministries the church can offer.

But it is impossible to have single adult leaders without a single adult ministry! We now turn to planning and building a single adult ministry at your church.

▲

CHAPTER 4

Starting a Single Adult Ministry from Scratch

A successful, effective single adult ministry begins with careful planning. The following ten steps are designed to help your church lay a solid foundation for ministering to single adults in your congregation and community.

TEN IMPORTANT STEPS TO TAKE

Step 1: Get Permission

Launch your singles program with as much support from the church as possible. Get permission from the power structure of the church (the pastor, the ruling elders, board, etc.). Do not attempt to organize a singles group without their blessing. Go to the power structure, present your idea, and get their permission and their blessing. You'll get a lot further with their help than without it.

Step 2: Survey Single Adults in the Church and Community

Conduct a survey to learn how many singles there are in the church. Include in your survey questions about age; whether there are children in the home; occupation and interests; and what kind of singles group they would enjoy. Learning the age range of single adults in your church will help you decide whether to organize your singles ministry around age groups. For example, if your survey shows the majority of single persons in your church are in their mid-thirties, you may wish to begin with a singles group mainly for this age group. Also find out how many single people live in your community. This information may be gathered from the U.S. Census Bureau or a private company that compiles demographics of your area according to age, sex, employment, education, household composition, marital status, and income. Such information will guide your planning and programming as your single adult ministry reaches out to singles in the community.

Duplicate or adapt the sample survey on the following page to use in your church. Feel free to add or delete any statements or questions on the survey. Remember, a survey is to help you assess the needs and interests of single adults in your church.

Step 3: Decide on the Type of Singles Group Your Church Needs

There are four kinds of singles groups to consider.

Sunday School

The focus of many single adult groups is the Sunday school class. Other programs and activities may happen throughout the week, but the major emphasis is the

SAMPLE SURVEY OF SINGLE ADULTS

Check the appropriate space to complete each statement.

I am ___divorced; ___widowed; ___have never been married.

I am in my ___20s ___30s ___40s ___50s ___60s and up.

How many children live at home with you? ___no children; ___one child; ___two children; ___three children; ___four or more children.

I am interested in attending one or more of the following kinds of singles groups:

___A Sunday school class for single adults.
___A singles group focused on social get-togethers and fellowship.
___A singles group with lots of activities away from the church.
___A singles Bible study on a week night.
___A singles group organized for my age group (as checked above).

I have been attending this church for ___less than 6 months; ___7 months to 1 year; ___2 to 5 years; ___6 to 10 years; ___10 or more years.

Complete the following statements:
My hobbies are

_____
_____
_____

My occupation is

_____

I would like to see a single adult ministry formed in this church because_____
_____
_____

singles class that meets on Sunday morning. Usually the focus of the Sunday school class is Bible study, but it should also provide an opportunity for singles to meet new people, and build vital community bonds with each other.

Midweek Religious Meeting

The main meeting for this group is one night during the week. It may meet as a Bible study, a koinonia or sharing group, or another kind of meeting with a religious emphasis. This group may or may not have a Sunday school for singles but the main event is the midweek meeting.

Midweek Life Enrichment Meeting

This group also meets during the week but the program consists of items of current interest to single adults. Most of the programs are presented by outside experts who talk about their field of expertise, followed by a group discussion of the presentation. Guest speakers may address the group on a variety of topics such as education, psychology, sports, religion, journalism, and entertainment. This group may not have a Sunday school for single adults, but the emphasis is on the midweek meeting.

The value of this type of meeting is that it offers a nonthreatening way for singles to come back to church who otherwise may have been alienated. Many first come to the enrichment programs during the week, then start to come to the class on Sundays. This is a great side-door approach to evangelism.

Off-Campus Sunday School

This group offers fellowship at a location other than the church, such as a meeting room in a nearby hotel or restaurant. The meeting is usually held at the same time as the regular Sunday school program.

The value of having Sunday school off-campus is that it often attracts single adults who have not been in church for years. However, there are a few disadvantages. The church or group must generally pay to rent a meeting room. Those who want to attend worship services afterward must drive to church. Single parents with young children must first drop them off at church before going to their off-campus Sunday school. In addition, the informal setting of an off-campus meeting room often lends itself to more of a social focus rather than a spiritual one.

Carefully weigh the pros and cons of organizing a Sunday school away from the church. Consult with the pastor, church leaders, and single members to make the best decision for your church and its singles ministry.

Step 4: Organize Brainstorming Meetings

Host a series of brainstorming meetings with interested singles to discuss organizing a singles class or group. The purpose of brainstorming meetings is to share your vision of a single adult class or group and to give singles equal time to respond with their thoughts on starting and participating in such a group. The time of the brainstorming meetings must be the same time that the class or group will meet once it's organized. The reason for this is to see who is available to assume leadership roles at that time. If they are available for the brainstorming meetings, they are probably available for the actual class or group. Announce two successive brainstorming meetings followed by the first actual class or group meeting. Prior to the first class, send out letters and make phone calls to everybody who attended the brainstorming sessions and to other positive, committed single persons in your church. Those who participated in the brainstorming, as well as other active singles in your church, will be the most likely candidates for leadership roles as the class or group grows.

After brainstorming, recruit several people to help you organize and launch the new class or group. You will need people to lead music, make announcements, welcome people, and so on. Later, after the group has been launched and solidified, organize elections. Do not have elections when the group or class first meets because they don't know each other well enough to elect people for a complete term.

Step 5: The First Class Session

Now you are ready to plan the first session of your group or class. Here are some suggestions for a successful first session.

- Invite a well-known Christian personality or expert to give a talk. This makes it that much more interesting to potential group members. They want to see and hear what a well-known person has to say.
- Send letters to all who attended the brainstorming meetings inviting them to attend the very first meeting of the new class and hear this person speak.
- Give this event plenty of publicity, both in church and in your community. (See Ch. 7, "The Value of Good Publicity," for further ideas.)

Step 6: Organize Planning Meetings

After the new class has met a few times, invite interested singles to come to a planning meeting. Planning meetings should meet monthly to plan future activities. Schedule these meetings early in the month so the planning group will have time to pull the information together to publish and distribute a newsletter or

printed calendar of activities. Distribute the calendar
the last Sunday of each month to promote the following
month's activities.

After your leaders get into the rhythm of planning for
the following months activities, encourage them to start
planning two months in advance.

For example, at the January planning meeting, after
formalizing plans for February, leaders outline activities for March. Assign leaders the task of getting
details and information for the activities they project for
March. Bring enough master calendars for all the members of the planning group to use. In January, for
example, the leader would bring in master calendars
that would have February on one side and March on the
other. The February side has the items scheduled on it
that were suggested at the December meeting. The
March side is blank unless leaders know of definite
commitments already arranged for that month.

Step 7: Create a Name for the Group

It is important for the singles group or class to have
a name. A name offers a sense of identity. Invite singles
to do some creative thinking and submit potential
names for their group. Award a prize to the person who
offers the best name. Discourage any name that has a
negative meaning or image to it. For example, one
singles class I know called themselves The Rejects.

The following are some catchy names I noticed in a
listing of singles groups by the Metrolina Singles
Magazine (of the Charlotte, North Carolina area).

SOFT (Singles Out For Togetherness)—an interdenominational Christian singles group.

SOLO (Singles Often Left Out)—a Christian
singles group in a nearby county.

Singles Blood Donor Club—single adults who donate blood or help with blood drives.

Sportin' Life—for singles who attend the various Charlotte, North Carolina, sporting events.

The Bachelor Club—a social group for never-married, career-oriented men.

Free Spirits—single adults interested in learning about and promoting Spirit Square and the arts community.

After selecting a name, ask a volunteer from the group or class to create a special logo for the group to be used in all your publicity and advertising.

Step 8: Create a Sense of Ownership

The brainstorming meetings encourage singles to take ownership of their group or class. Ownership occurs when they begin speaking of the group as their group. Singles support and attend programs in which they have a vested interest. Therefore, encourage them to organize, implement, and control their own activities. Ownership of the planning process and programs is a sign of a vital, healthy, single adult ministry.

Step 9: Develop a Mission Statement

Once singles demonstrate signs of ownership of their group or class, invite them to develop a mission statement. A mission statement enables the group to think through their purpose or reason for being. A good mission statement answers the following questions:

Who are we?

Whom do we serve?

What service do we provide?

Divide large singles groups into small groups and let each group answer a question. Then reassemble the small groups and let each group offer their answers to each question. You could use an overhead projector, large charts, or newsprint tacked to the walls to write down each group's answers for all to see. Assimilate the best of the small groups' answers into one comprehensive answer for each of the three questions. Developing a mission statement in this way produces bonding among single adults.

Once the group agrees on their mission statement, read it occasionally in group meetings or print it periodically in the singles newsletter. This will keep singles focused on their mission.

The following is an example of the single adults mission statement at Countryside Christian Church in Mission, Kansas.

Who Are We?

We are the adult singles ministry of Countryside Christian Church, an outreach-oriented group of dynamic, loving singles of all ages. We represent diverse interests, lifestyles, and socio-economic backgrounds and yet share common Christian values.

Whom Do We Serve?

We serve single adults who are unmarried, divorced, or widowed. And we serve their children in the Kansas City area.

What Service Do We Provide?

We provide an ongoing Christian ministry through an active, supportive, and nurturing fellowship, whereby the single person can grow spiritually, socially, and emotionally through meaningful activities, service projects, and other events.

Use the following form to create a mission statement for the single adult ministry in your church. Once the ministry has completed their mission statement, remember to regularly publicize the mission statement among group members. Also distribute the mission statement to clergy, staff, and the congregation.

OUR SINGLE ADULT MINISTRY'S MISSION STATEMENT

Who are we?

_____

_____

_____

_____

_____

_____

Whom do we serve?

_____

_____

_____

_____

_____

_____

What service do we provide?

_____

_____

_____

_____

_____

Step 10: Plan a Really Big Event

Now that the single adult ministry is organized, experienced in the planning process, has a sense of ownership about its activities, and has a name and logo, plan a big celebration for the single adults in your community. There are two reasons for doing this: A celebration event builds a sense of togetherness among the members of the single adult ministry as they work on the project, and working together planning and executing a big event gives a great feeling of accomplishment. All the publicity the single adult group generates to promote this big event tells singles in your community that the single adult group is organized and in business to help meet their needs. Periodically plan big events as an outreach activity to singles in your community.

DEVELOPING A BALANCED PROGRAM

Now that your churche's single adult ministry is off the ground, concentrate on developing balanced programs and activities. Imagine single adult ministry as a wheel with five spokes. Each spoke is a program that contributes to a well-rounded, successful single adult ministry. Not everyone will be attracted to every spoke. Some spokes attract certain people, while other spokes attract others. To paraphrase a popular saying, "It's different *spokes* for different folks."

Spoke 1—Spiritual Programs

Church-based singles groups need not apologize for offering various types of spiritual growth programs for single adults. Such spiritual programs include a singles Sunday morning fellowship or Sunday school class; a weeknight Bible study group; a prayer circle or prayer chain, and annual singles retreats. You could explore creating a section in the pews of the church sanctuary that is unofficially known as the singles section, which allows single individuals to worship together with their "extended family."

Spoke 2—Support Groups

Occasionally everyone benefits from a support group of one kind or another. Balanced singles programs offer support groups to meet special needs of group members. Grief recovery, divorce recovery, and single parenting are a few examples of support groups a well-rounded ministry may offer. (See Ch. 12, "Support Groups.")

Spoke 3—Social Opportunities

Fellowship opportunities are critical to all programs. Many singles hunger for wholesome adult fellowship. All programs must provide plenty of time to mix and mingle with each other. Also plan special social activities whose only purpose is to have fun. A few ideas for socials are clubhouse parties, VCR parties; potlucks and picnics, dances, trips and tours, and table game parties. Also organize social activities around the various fine arts: Go to the art gallery, the museum, or the symphony together. (See Ch. 13, "Activities.")

Spoke 4—Recreational Opportunities

Plan a variety of sports and recreational opportunities for single adults. These range from team sports (such as volleyball and softball) to things singles can do in smaller groups (such as ping-pong, jogging, miniature golf, regular golf, skating, bowling, camping, canoeing). Also organize trips to spectator sports like professional football or college basketball.

Spoke 5—Service Projects

Plan programs and activities that help other people. A balanced single adult ministry reaches out to help others. (See Ch. 14, "Service Projects.")

A healthy, growing single adult ministry offers all five kinds of programs throughout the year. Varied programs fit together to meet the needs of all single adults in your church and your community. So begin to think about the activities in these five categories that will appeal to your group.

SINGLES GROUPS AND SMALL CHURCHES

It is far more difficult to form a singles group at a small church or in a small town than in larger churches or metropolitan areas. However, there is a tremendous need among singles in rural areas or in small churches for fellowship with one another.

You don't have to belong to a "megachurch" to bring singles together; small churches can develop successful single adult ministries too. Following the general guidelines below will help your small church minister to the needs of single adults attending your church as well as the needs of singles in your community.

To Begin With . . .

Convince your church to commit money to help underwrite the single adult ministry. Set aside a small budget to cover promotional costs in publicizing the group's activities and events. You may need funds for refreshments at the classes or meetings. You will definitely need money to photocopy letters and calendars for the group. Consider what it will take to get your group going, and see if the church can help to finance those plans.

Then ask several key single members of the church (though they may be involved in other church classes or fellowships) to make a six-month commitment to contact singles about forming a single adult ministry. Their support is invaluable in getting the program off the ground. After six months, those key people are free to return to their former classes, if they wish, or they may remain in the singles group and continue to help build the ministry. Many will choose to remain.

Consider choosing one group or class listed below to begin your single adult ministry.

Sunday School Class

If possible, develop a singles class. Ask some of your single adults involved in other classes to take a leave of absence from other duties to help start the singles Sunday school class. Invite interesting speakers and plan solid teaching times. Make the topics relevant to your group.

Evening Community-Based Program

An evening program will draw more single adults than a Sunday school class. Hold meetings in someone's home or a casual location within the church. If you keep things informal and relaxed, you will attract more "unchurched" single adults.

Combine with Other Churches

Organize a single adult ministry made up of singles from several small local churches. You will have more singles participating in programs and activities. And working together with other churches offers more resources for ministry. Single adult groups or classes may rotate among area churches or establish a permanent meeting location at one church, with other churches participating in programs there.

Don't Forget to Advertise

Once you've decided when, where, and how to begin your single adults ministry, be sure to contact your local community newspaper about free publicity. Small-town newspapers will often support local church activities with publicity and free advertising. You won't lose a thing by asking. (For more suggestions on how to promote and advertise, see Ch. 7 on publicity.)

A few years ago I received a mailing from a small, rural church in Kansas. Some of the single adult members of this church—Zion United Methodist in Robinson, Kansas—attended a leadership seminar I conducted. Several months later, they sent me their monthly newsletter containing information on their upcoming singles conference. I enjoyed their mailing and read about the fine activities that small church had planned for single adults in their area. You could do the same kind of newsletter.

While every small church might not be able to develop an ongoing calendar of activities for their single adults, it's good to know that some are developing successful countywide programs like the Zion church.

WAYS TO HELP INTEGRATE THE SINGLES MINISTRY INTO THE LIFE OF THE CHURCH

One of the criticisms often aimed at singles groups is that they are only a social group and don't really care about their connection with the sponsoring church. Let's examine this further.

There are always single adults who attend the group

or class only because they want to meet new friends and/or they like the activities. These singles could care less about the things of the Spirit or affiliating with the church. Some of these singles will never be involved in the church at large. But don't be discouraged. There are others who want deep spiritual nurture. Encourage these members to affiliate with the church and participate in other ministries.

Many single adults do crave a deeper walk with the Lord and a closer relationship with the church. Some were active in church at one time in their lives, slipped away for whatever reasons, and have now returned to the church with a real hunger to become involved again. Help these people make solid connections with the fuller life of the church. Church members who are a little suspicious of the singles program will be convinced of its value as a ministry when they see singles getting involved with the rest of the church.

There are some concrete ways you can integrate the singles group into the life of the church.

- Let the single adult ministry sponsor a major event for the entire church. This may be something as simple as an ice cream social or organizing a major service project, such as feeding Thanksgiving dinner to underprivileged families. If your group is not large enough to do this, singles may join other groups in the church to plan large activities.
- Encourage the single adult ministry to form their own drama group, choir, or musical ensemble and occasionally perform in worship services.
- Get permission from the pastor or church board for the singles group to plan and celebrate an entire worship service once a year as the church recognizes Singles Day.
- Encourage single adults to attend the worship

services and special holiday services during the year.

- Invite single adults, especially ones who are church members, to attend various church business and committee meetings whenever appropriate.
- One of the best ways to integrate single adults into the life of the church is through education. Help singles understand the various functions of the church by inviting various staff and department heads to come to a singles class or other meeting and give a brief description of what that department does and how it affects single adults.

For example, ask the head of the trustees to explain how that department oversees the physical building and the purchase of new office equipment. This person could describe some of the church's expansion plans for the next few years. Ask the head deacon or elder to explain that board's function and the style of church government your church uses. The head of the adult education department could describe other adult Sunday school classes in the church. The latter is of particular value to single adults, many of whom eventually marry and move out of the singles class into another class within the church. If they know there are other options for learning and ministry, they will stay in the church rather than quit at the time of their marriage.

Acquainting single people with church leaders demonstrates that the singles group wants to be a part of the church—not a separate entity. It also helps church leaders become better acquainted with the singles program and with the members themselves.

One such talk a month by a staff person or department head should be sufficient. If possible, begin with a department head who was once in the singles class. Or begin with the department that has the most bearing on single adult life in the church, such as the adult education department. Invite all departments to speak to the single adult ministry. Individuals in the group may volunteer to help on a department committee once they understand a department's function.

That covers the general issues involved in planning and launching a single adult ministry. Next we turn to a deeper examination of organization: developing a planning process; creating solid, unified programs; discovering publicity opportunities; and financing your single adult ministry.

▲

CHAPTER 5

Electing Officers and Organizing Committees

As the single adult group elects officers and form committees, they will begin to feel a sense of ownership among themselves for the programs, activities, and the general ministry. But don't encourage elections in the very beginning; wait until the members know each other better. You should serve as primary leader in the first few months to insure that the group is headed in the right direction. The first elected officers are crucial to the future of the group. Let candidates who have demonstrated loyalty and leadership in the group rise to the occasion.

ESTABLISHING OFFICES

Most singles groups need only the standard four officers: president, vice president, secretary, and treasurer. Some groups prefer to substitute the word moderator for president.

In addition to the elected officers, the group needs committees to handle assignments for socials, service projects, music and worship, visitor follow-up, and so on. The reason for having a number of committees in a single adult ministry is to get as many people involved as possible. The more people involved, the greater the ownership of and participation in the programs and activities.

A simple organization should work for most average-sized classes. However, if your singles group also has several single adult Sunday school classes, each class should have its own set of officers and committees. Groups with multiple classes often have a singles council, which functions as the governing body for all the singles classes. The council is composed of one or more of the elected officers from each class.

By sharing the ministry, you share the joy of serving together and creating a sense of ownership and togetherness.

Distribute a clear written description of duties to each person serving in office. It would be a good idea for the rest of the singles group to know these duties too.

Then establish an executive board. I suggest all officers comprise the executive board. Each officer oversees several committees (to be discussed later). Though I suggest two vice presidents, their duties may be combined into one if that would fit your ministry better.

Members of the Executive Board and Their Responsibilities

President

The president presides over the Sunday school class, the planning meetings, and all other official meetings of the single adult ministry.

Vice President

This officer is might consider this person responsible for primarily spiritual and emotional direction. This vice president recommends to the executive board chairpersons for the following committees: spiritual life, music and worship, sharing and caring, greeters, and service projects. This vice president is also responsible for the proper functioning of these committees and serves as the president pro tem in the absence of the president.

Second Vice President

This vice president's responsibilities tend to fall in the social and recreational areas. This vice president recommends to the executive board chairpersons for the following committees: sports/recreation, socials/dinners, family activities, and trips/tours. This person is responsible for the proper functioning of these committees and serves as the president pro tem in the absence of the president and the first vice president.

Treasurer

The treasurer is responsible for the collection and recording of funds for various singles events and activities. The treasurer should furnish a monthly financial report to the executive board. This person recommends to the executive board a chairperson for the fundraising committee and is responsible for the proper functioning of that committee.

Secretary

The secretary records the actions of the executive board at planning meetings, and reads the minutes of previous meetings. The secretary, in charge of communicating with the executive board and the group at large, recommends to the executive board a chairperson for the singles newsletter and publicity committee and is responsible for the proper functioning of these committees.

The Nominating Committee

When nominating officers, *never, never, never* pit one candidate for office against another. Doing so opens the door to hurt feelings and division. Another reason for not pitting one collection of candidates against another is that most groups don't have enough well-qualified people to fill one slate, let alone two. The nominating committee should select only one person for each office and present these individuals to the group for approval.

In the beginning, the singles leader or staff person should appoint three persons to serve on the nominating committee. After the single adult ministry has been launched and growing for several years, recommend a policy that all past presidents or moderators serve as the nominating committee.

When the nominating committee meets, they should choose a candidate for the president's position first. This encourages a choice among best leaders to be the president. After selecting a presidential candidate, the committee nominates the remaining officers. Finally, the committee contacts all the candidates to see whether they would serve if elected. The committee reads the candidates the responsibilities of office so they know what is expected of them. Then the committee asks each individual to serve in that office if elected.

Qualifications for Office

Before selecting anyone to lead the group long-term, the single adult ministry leader must establish some qualifications for office. Candidates must be selected on their leadership ability rather than simple popularity. But where do you begin to look for these leaders? Normally, the pool of qualified officer candidates comes from various committees in the church at large. Look for single adults who have performed well on committees before; they are most likely to be officer material. You can tell that a person is qualified for office when he or she has demonstrated an ability to handle past assignments. However, if an individual was unable to fulfill his or her responsibilities, the individual is not a likely candidate for a more responsible level of leadership.

You should also consider whether the candidate is interested in the kinds of activities he or she would be responsible for. The individual's current involvements will give you a clue about the jobs they are good at and enjoy the most.

Some church singles groups require the president be a member of the church. Other groups require all their officers to be church members. Big ministries with a large pool of qualified persons often insist that all committee persons join the church.

Another qualification to consider is the candidate's personal life. Do candidates exemplify leadership? Do they seem to have deep spiritual commitment? Do candidates attract people? Do they have a positive attitude most of the time? Do candidates have hidden agendas for serving, such as being more interested in finding a mate than caring for the whole group? Do candidates have their own lives fairly well in order? Do they handle their current responsibilities well? Are they good role models? Answering these questions will help produce the best officers for your single adult ministry.

The Elections

Announce the nominees in the singles newsletter, then conduct the elections about a month before the term begins. This gives the new officers time to select their committee chairs. Should new nominations come from the floor, accept the nomination only if the person being nominated gives his or her verbal consent (in writing if they are not there on the day of the elections).

Seek a motion from the group to elect the nominees by acclamation. But if an actual vote is needed, do it by secret ballot. There is nothing evil or wrong about secret ballots. Secret ballots allow voters to express their true thoughts, which they might not care to do publicly. And secret ballots may save embarrassment among the candidates. Have secret ballots prepared in advance in case you don't get the motion for acclamation.

Officers by Application

Most single adult groups elect their officers. But there is another approach to consider. This idea comes from The Christian Single by Dianne Swaim, director of the single adult ministry at Immanuel Baptist Church in Little Rock, Arkansas.[1]

In her article entitled "A Functioning Single Adult Council," Swaim writes, "We established the means for entrance into the single adult council to be by application rather than popular vote. But those chosen to serve are presented to their classmates for affirmation, which preserves the democratic process." As a result of officers by application,

> We have members who have a strong desire to work, who are committed to meeting the needs of single adults, . . . and who will be responsible in attending meetings, chairing committees, and promoting activities within the group. They serve because they really want to, rather than because they were elected.

Swaim says that certain requirements should be included in the application. "If there were no requirements, the result would be as irresponsible as the election may be. Criteria should not be simple, but strict enough to weed out those who are not serious." Her requirements include a statement of personal salvation, a knowledge of spiritual gifts, and membership in the church.

Finally, a contract statement may be included, signed, and dated. Our statement is simple but inclusive: "I will agree to be faithful in attendance at all council meetings, to chair one or more committees during my tenure, to faithfully support the church as a whole and the Single Adult Ministry, and to consider myself a vital part of the leadership team during the time on the council."

Swaim points out that while council members chair the committees, others in the single adult group make up the working committee. This gets more people involved and allows for leadership traits to be developed in future officers.

COMMITTEE APPOINTMENTS

Newly elected officers appoint their own committees. Hold a joint session of all newly elected officers to appoint committee chairs. This will promote interaction and keep them from selecting all the same people for a variety of committees.

Committee Chairs and Their Responsibilities

Committee chairs regularly attend Sunday school and all planning meetings. They are also responsible for the smooth functioning of their respective committees.

Spiritual Life Committee

This group plans and oversees the spiritual life of the

single adult ministry, specifically organizing class devotions, retreats, workshops, and seminars regarding issues of the spiritual life.

Music Committee

The committee chair is responsible for organizing the music in Sunday school and at any other occasions requiring music. The chair also plans music activities for the group, such as sing-alongs and Christmas caroling.

Fundraising Committee

The committee chair plans and recommends various fundraising projects during the year. The chair is responsible for the proper functioning of the projects once approved.

Greeting Committee

The committee chair is responsible for appointing monthly greeters who organize the welcome table in Sunday school class. The greeter arrives at least fifteen minutes early to set up the table with materials and returns the materials to storage after class. The chair lines up various individuals on the committee who rotate the responsibility of greeting on a monthly basis. All persons on the greeting committee should be available each Sunday to help visitors feel welcome and included.

Sharing and Caring Committee

The chair is constantly aware of the unique needs of group members and mobilizes resources to meet those needs. For example, helping a member move; buying wedding gifts; sending flowers to those hospitalized or when a death occurs. You might also consider setting up a prayer committee or a prayer chain within this committee to intercede specifically for needs within the singles group.

Dinners Committee

The chair oversees the planning, purchase, and preparation of food for activities. For example, monthly social dinners; LEO's (Let's Eat Out) activities; and occasional picnics.

Service Committee

The chair searches out, plans and oversees the execution of various outreach or service projects approved by the executive board.

Recreation/Sports Committee

The chair organizes and develops various types of recreational/sports activities, whether a single event or a league (as in a sports league).

Social Committee

The chair is responsible for the planning and implementation of various social activities approved by the planning committee. For example, house parties; holiday parties; theme parties and other socials.

Newsletter Committee

The chair is responsible for helping collect material for the monthly newsletter, typing it, and mailing it, unless office staff is available to do that.

Family Activities

The chair searches out local events and activities suitable for single- parent children. The chair also makes the group more aware of how it can occasionally involve these children in its regular activities. The committee also plans an annual event such as a retreat or games night for the children of the single parents.

Trips and Tours Committee

The chair researches and plans various trips or tours locally as well as overnight trips.

Follow-up Committee

The chair is responsible for the immediate phone follow-up of all persons who have visited the class or group as well as those regular members who have missed four or more Sundays or events. The committee also telephones recent visitors to invite them to special events.

Terms of Office

A major question among singles leaders is the length of terms of elected officers and committee persons. I conducted a small survey in 1989 among singles leaders concerned about this issue. I asked about their officers: "How long is the term of office?" Of those who responded, their answers included:

No officers:	11
6-month terms:	14
9-month terms:	01
12-month terms:	42
Other:	39

I think the ideal term of officers and committee chairs is nine months, but that is often impractical. Six months is too short and twelve months is often too long. However, my experience and the survey showed that the most typical length of a term is twelve months.

There are disadvantages to twelve-month terms. It is

often psychologically difficult for people to commit to serve for a whole year. And they often burnout halfway through their term.

To fight both these disadvantages I suggest asking people to serve for a period of six months with an option to renew their commitment for the next six months. Send a motivational letter to all officers and committee chairs during the first six months of their term and charge them up to finish the balance of the year with the same enthusiasm they started with. Also, include in the letter an option for any who might wish to resign to do so. This gives them a graceful way to exit at the end of six months if they need to.

Limit the number of terms a person can serve in office to one. This encourages new people to get involved. If the same people continue to serve in the same positions, it doesn't motivate new people to exercise leadership. Another advantage to limiting terms in office is that someone who's not doing the job well won't be around for too long.

A final advantage to limiting terms is that it prevents officers and committee chairs from becoming stale and losing interest. It encourages them to move around and serve in different capacities. Bringing in new officers and committee chairs also keeps the planning group fresh and dynamic.

CHAPTER **6**

▲

The Planning Process

Once the single adult ministry has elected officers and organized committees, begin monthly officers' meetings and planning meetings to outline the activities of the group. Officers' and planning meetings may be scheduled on the same day, one meeting succeeding the other. It helps if you schedule these meetings to fall at the same time each month so participants can reserve time for these meetings. Meet early enough in the month so that officers and committees have time to finalize all details and write, print, and distribute the monthly activities calendar during the last general group meeting of the month.

THE OFFICERS' MEETING (THE EXECUTIVE BOARD)

The officers' meeting is the time when the singles leader, minister, or staff meets with the officers to discuss matters that affect the overall function of the group. The officers may meet immediately before the planning meeting. Only the officers attend this meeting. The singles leader presides.

Use this time to raise issues and discuss ideas with

the officers, such as: how to make the single adults more visible to the congregation, what the group could do to help a fellow member whose house burned down, evaluating current teaching materials, and how the class responded when we had a guest speaker. When the officers come to a decision on these matters, they present those ideas and issues in the planning meeting which follows.

THE PLANNING MEETING

The purpose of the planning meeting is to discuss general business and plan for future activities of the group. It tends to run longer than the officers' meeting. Doing business at this meeting prevents using up valuable time in Sunday school or at the regular meeting of the whole group. Visitors and peripheral members do not appreciate planning and business discussions during regular group meetings.

Should your church have only one single adult class or group, the group president presides over the planning meeting. Should your church have a class and a group, both presidents alternate presiding. In multiclass churches or those with a singles council, the council decides who should preside.

Officers, committee chairpersons, and those serving on committees should attend the planning meeting. However, to keep planning from being an exclusive activity, extend an open invitation to anyone who has ideas for programs or events. The secretary keeps an attendance record at this meeting. (This record comes in handy when discussing future officers and evaluating their dependability.)

The planning meeting must follow a standard order. I suggest the following order: an opening prayer, the secretary's report, the treasurer's report, committee reports, the leader's report, discussion of old business and new business, and planning future programs and activities. Everyone will appreciate it if the meeting is orderly, democratic, and efficient.

As people enter the planning meeting, the leader distributes copies of the planning calendar for the month you want to work on. That calendar may already have printed on it some of the regular monthly activities (for example, the monthly dinner out on the third Thursday and the service project on the fourth Tuesday) as well as any other events the group has already agreed to do that month.

As the president directs the planning process, each person attending should have an opportunity to present ideas to the rest of the group. If an activity is approved, enter it on the calendar and assign someone to write a description of the event for the editor of the newsletter. The calendar and activity descriptions should be completed at the meeting and turned in to the newsletter editor. If the planning meeting is scheduled in the first half of the month, there is time to get further details and work on the event descriptions after the meeting and still hand it over to the editor before the deadline.

Distribute the form on page 76 to members of the planning committee. Each person sponsoring an activity completes this form and presents it during the planning meeting. A completed Activity Form helps answer any questions the planning committee may have about an event. It also provides all necessary information about an activity for publicity.

MARCH

Sunday	Monday	Tuesday	Wednesday	Thursday	Friday	Saturday
	1	2	3 Birthday Dinner at Furr's Cafeteria	4	5	6
7	8 Planning Meeting	9	10	11	12	13 Roller Skating, PIC=Bill
14	15	16	17	18 Dinner out, PIC=Julia	19	20
21 Palm Sunday	22	23	24 Anniversary Dinner PIC=Mark	25	26	27 Movie at the Mall, PIC=Alan
28 Easter Potluck Lunch at Sue's	29	30 Service Project PIC=Anne	31			

ANNUAL EVENTS

January	February	March	April
Installation of officers (1/2); Volleyball league	Valentine Banquet (2/3); Volleyball league; Snow skiing in Colorado (2/9-12)	Anniversary Dinner (3/24); Easter potluck lunch (3/28)	Spring retreat (4/10-12); Special Olympics (4/21-24)

May	June	July	August
Softball league; Memorial Day Picnic (5/31)	Softball league; Canoe trip (6/12-13); Ice cream concert (6/25)	4th of July swim party and cookout; Softball league; Music in the Parks; Crown Center concerts	Start selling coupon books; Theatre in the Parks; Lake trip (8/13-15)

September	October	November	December
Labor Day Picnic (9/6); Dinner/Dance (9/18)	Fall Retreat (10/1-3); Hayride (10/16); Haloween Party; Volleyball league	Nominations (11/7); Thanksgiving brunch (11/25); Hanging of the Greens (11/28); Plaza Lighting Ceremony (11/26); Volleyball league	Elections (12/5); Festival of Light (12/13-17); Caroling; Volleyball league

ACTIVITY FORM

Name of activity:_____

Date(s):_____Time(s): _____

Exact location and address: _____

Indicate special directions to the location of the activity (if necessary, attach a map to this form): _____

_____

Are children invited? Yes No

Is child care provided? Yes No

If yes, indicate location of child care: _____

Cost of the activity: Individual price Group price _____

Price for adults _____

Price for children _____

No charge

Food is involved: Yes No

If yes, what time will we begin eating? _____

Do participants bring food? Yes No

If yes, please indicate what kind of food participants are to bring to the activity. _____

Reservations are required: Yes No

If yes, the deadline for reservations is _____

Make reservations by calling:

Name:

Phone(s): Home:_____ Work: _____

The activity organizer(s): _____

Name _____

Phone(s) Home:_____Work: _____

Name _____

Phone(s) Home:_____Work: _____

Describe appropriate dress for this activity: _____

_____

Indicate a contingency plan (in case the activity must be canceled or rescheduled due to weather, etc.) _____

Comments or special instructions: _____

Date when the details and plans for the activity will be finished and in place: _____

Please write a brief, inviting description of the activity below. This description will be printed in the newsletter and/or other promotional materials. Please type or print clearly: _____

_____

Thank you for your help!

PLANNING TIPS

The Value of a PIC- "Person in Charge"

Our singles group appoints a person to be in charge (or PIC) of our various singles activities, particularly those we hold away from the church building such as Kansas City Royal's baseball games, miniature golf, LEOs (Let's Eat Out get-togethers), one-day trips, picnics, or concerts. As the single adult leader, I am usually in charge of the big events like the retreats and most of the programs held at the church. But for activities outside the church, we make good use of other PICs.

There are two reasons to assign a PIC to each activity. First, as the singles leader I cannot possibly attend all of our activities; even if I could, I would not always want to be in charge. And second, having someone else in charge enables us to groom new leaders or give current leaders some responsibility. Our group is filled with many responsible people and being a PIC is a way to demonstrate leadership skills.

People agree to be PICs in advance. They either volunteer at the monthly planning meeting or are otherwise asked to be a PIC before the calendar is printed. If no one volunteers to be in charge, don't schedule that activity.

PICs have four responsibilities.

1. They welcome all who come to the activity and introduce the visitors.

2.   They are to make sure the activity occurs as
      printed and publicized.
3.   Each PIC's phone number (home and work) is
      printed with their activities, and he or she
      answers questions regarding that activity.
4.   Since many of our activities are away from the
      church building, the PIC meets those who come
      to the church to carpool and insures that the
      group leaves on time for the activity.

In short, the PIC has the responsibility to see that the
activity is carried out as planned by the planning committee.

A Cure for Stale Thinking

If your planning process is in a rut, schedule a potluck
supper followed by a brainstorming session with
everyone throwing in ideas for new and exciting activities and programs. This is a special meeting,
separate from all other meetings.

Begin by inviting all who are interested to voice their
ideas. Three simple brainstorming rules foster a sense
of freedom and willingness to offer new ideas:

1.   No one is allowed to criticize either the idea or
      the person making the idea. When discussing the
      pros and cons of an idea, be objective and do not
      criticize the person who offered the idea.
2.   Continually encourage people to throw in new
      ideas. The more ideas the better.
3.   It is all right for one idea to overlap another; one
      idea can be very similar to another idea. Come
      up with as many variations of an idea as you
      want.

A good brainstorming session usually cures stale
thinking and planning. And it is often a time of fun and
fellowship.

Two-Month Planning

One anxiety in planning sessions is how to come up with enough appropriate activities for the following month. One way to reduce this anxiety is to plan two months in advance. In other words, instead of planning only for the immediate next month's activities, plan the month after next and continue to do so all year.

Once all the details for the next month's calendar are finalized, sketch out activities for the month. After that if the group likes those ideas, enter them on the planning calendar for that month. Assign someone to get the details for those activities and to report the information at the next planning meeting.

For example, assume it is now January and we are in our meeting to plan February activities. Once you have finished planning February, suggest programs and activities for March and ask specific members to get more details on each item. At the February planning meeting, those persons assigned to get details for the March activities report on their findings. The group either accepts or rejects activities depending on the details submitted. Write each accepted activity on the calendar. If there are some holes in the month, consider new ideas. Once March is planned, then the group outlines activities for April and assigns people to check out the details for those proposed activities.

When planning two months ahead, the leader copies a large calendar of the second month on the back side of the coming month's calendar. These calendars are invaluable aids in planning activities (see sample in this chapter).

Annual Calendar

Another helpful tool is the annual calendar of activities. This calendar is a one-page document with twelve squares. It contains the major events the group traditionally does during those months. Such events may include elections and installation, the Valentine Banquet, the spring retreat, the annual canoe trip, anything you do every year.

Such a calendar guides your planning meeting. It helps the planners remember what the group usually does during certain months. And it helps individuals plan their own schedules by seeing ahead of time what they may want to attend. For example, if the group knows that you historically plan a canoe trip the third weekend in June, some people may plan their vacation another time so they can go on the canoe trip.

Annual Training Session

If possible, schedule a half-day training session for all new officers and committee heads. The best time for this is shortly after all elections and appointments have been made. The training session goes over the job descriptions and planning process guidelines. It also builds camaraderie among your newly elected and appointed people.

Plan the training session a month or so in advance and have it at a nearby retreat center. Also, to encourage attendance, provide lunch and child care. But arrange to have the children cared for at another convenient location—not where the session is being held. Single parents will be less distracted.

A good planning process increases the level of enjoyment and fun for everyone involved in the single adult ministry. And it encourages the development of good leadership skills in many single adults. So develop good planning early in the ministry—and have fun!

Vary Your Programs

Once you have your planning process in place, you

must start thinking about what kind of events and programs to do! The majority of all programs for single adults fit into one of the following categories: entertainment, educational, religious or spiritual, supportive, social, or recreational. Good programming includes activities in all of these categories. People like variety. And the same is true of programs offered by single adult groups. Groups that become stale are groups that don't vary their programs.

You may offer some programs all the time because of the continuing needs of your group. For example, a single-parent support group should exist as long as there are people who need it. Or your single adult should always continue Sunday school class because everyone has spiritual needs. But even with these two examples, you need to keep them fresh by varying the routine occasionally. The single-parent support group may simply change the arrangement of the room or host a social activity once or twice a month. You can freshen up the Sunday school class by inviting different teachers occasionally.

Entertainment programs help members relax and get away from the daily grind. Educational programs stretch the mind a little and expand horizons on certain subjects. Spiritual programs offer a foundation for living in Christ. And support groups help when foundations begin to crumble.

Remember, it may be safe to keep the status quo, but it can also kill your group. Groups that are dynamic will risk doing something new and different once in a while. Offering programs from each category keep the single adult ministry fresh and growing.

Good Program Ideas

I am often asked about program ideas and speakers for singles groups. While I am happy to recommend

specific ideas or people, I usually offer the following tips
so groups can generate their own repertoire of program
ideas for the future.

Community Organizations

Invite speakers from the community. There are community organizations in your area that can refer you to
speakers such as nurses or other health professionals;
Salvation Army representatives; people from Alcoholics
Anonymous and other Twelve Step programs; college or
seminary professors; family or school counselors; hospital or military chaplains; job placement specialists;
retirement specialists; hospice workers; politicians in
city and government agencies; mental health professionals; local authors; and other singles leaders.

Films and Videos

Educational films and videos are often available free
of charge through local libraries and corporations.
Topics range from energy to ecology, from health to
technology. For a catalog of educational materials offered by one company, send a postcard to Modern Talking Picture Service, 500 Park Street North, St.
Petersburg, Florida, 33709 (phone: 813-541-7571).

Religious films and videos are also available through
companies such as EcuFilm, 810 12th Avenue South,
Nashville, Tennessee 37203 (1-800-251-4091) and local
church resource centers.

Of course, the commercial video stores have a wide
selection of videos to rent. Though most of their videos
are Hollywood movies, most establishments have
educational and religious videos to rent too.

Calendar Themes

Most seasons of the year have certain special days
and holidays. Many of these are religious in origin and

lend themselves to communicating biblical principles through special programs. The calendar itself suggests lots of ideas for programs and social activities. Here are a few suggestions.

Apart from New Year's Day, the first national holiday of the new year is Martin Luther King, Jr.'s Birthday observance on January 15. On or near this day, plan a program dealing with injustice, racial inequities, or review some of the great martyrs in history. Or plan a program around personal dreams and hopes for a better world and read excerpts of Martin Luther King, Jr.'s famous "I Have A Dream" speech.

Plan a program about St. Valentine, his imprisonment for his faith, and the beginning of Valentine's Day. This is also a good time for classes to think about new ways to love and care for each other.

President's Day honors two of our nation's greatest leaders: George Washington and Abraham Lincoln. Invite a speaker to review each man's public and private life; guide a discussion regarding some of the legends about each; examine how their characters and beliefs were influenced by Christian principles.

Plan a program around the legend of St. Patrick, patron saint of Ireland. Explain that Patrick loved the shamrock because the three tiny leaves reminded him of the Trinity. Talk about contemporary saints who are doing good works and helping others (like Mother Teresa).

Plan a program teaching the historical basis for all the activities related to Easter—Lent, Ash Wednesday, Palm Sunday, Holy Week, Good Friday, and Easter Sunday.

Present a brief biography of Columbus, including his trials and his strong religious convictions.

Discuss the history of Halloween. This is a good

holiday to plan a program for single adults and their children.

On Veteran's Day, invite a veteran to talk about patriotism and what it means to be a loyal American.

Re-enact the first Thanksgiving, complete with turkey dinner, and focus on all the things you all have to be thankful for.

Christmas is the perfect time of year to again focus on the birth of our Lord.

Yellow Pages

Thumb through your local Yellow Pages and get ideas from the various headings and categories. For example, the planning meeting may develop programs just using the A listing in the Yellow Pages: accountants (on tax and financial matters); adoption agencies; air conditioning (on heating and air conditioning tips); aircraft/airlines (tour the local airport or overhaul base); alcoholism; animal hospitals (on the care and feeding of animals); antiques (the difference between antiques and junk); apartments (landlord and tenant laws); arbitration services (conflict resolution); arts and crafts shops (the latest craze in crafts); athletic organizations; attorneys (a two- or three-part program covering different aspects of the law each time); auctioneers (plan a live auction to raise funds); automobiles (various programs concerning used car buying, minor car repair, or the case for leasing).

The next time your ideas run dry, just pick up the telephone book and "let your fingers do the walking" for new and interesting programs.

Local Speakers' Bureaus

Many cities have speakers' bureaus operated by the Chamber of Commerce, the library, the police department, the school district, hospitals, or mental health agencies. Check with each bureau for a list of speakers and topics.

Speakers' Exchanges

Peggy O'Keef of Phoenix started a speakers' exchange to assist local single adult groups in that area with speakers for their programs. As the program chairperson for a local singles group, she had a lot of experience in booking speakers for singles programs.

To launch her speakers' exchange, she asked all the single adult groups in the area to call her with names of good speakers they had used in the past. She also invited interested beginning and experienced speakers to contact her.

Peggy now has between forty and fifty speakers on file, representing a wide range of subjects. She has located motivational speakers, travel agents, economists, aviators, police officers, tax attorneys, and various government representatives. This is Peggy's community service, and there are no fees for using the exchange. Your single adult ministry may consider consulting or setting up a similar speakers' bureau for churches in your area.

Local Celebrities

Make a list of local celebrities by recording the names of persons mentioned in your local media. Sometimes media people themselves are able to make appearances and give talks.

How to Recruit Celebrities

Speaking of celebrities, have you ever wanted a celebrity to be a guest speaker but didn't think he or she would come without a big honorarium? Some big celebrities are very busy and command top dollar for an appearance—but you never know until you ask. While most celebrities do charge for appearances, they often make exceptions for churches and charities, particularly if they are Christians with a message to share. I have booked a number of celebrities over the years and have often been surprised at how quickly some of them accepted and offered to come for free!

Many celebrities have unlisted phone numbers. Call or write a letter to your celebrity's workplace. Some professional sports teams have a speakers' bureau of athletes who make guest appearances. Political figures also like to make public appearances because it gets them out among their constituents. And the closer you are to elections, the more likely they are to accept your invitation.

When you ask celebrities to give a speech, make it easy on them. Pick a topic familiar to the celebrity. Ask what talks or speeches the celebrity has readily available and are suitable for your situation.

If your celebrity is not available now, she or he may be in a few months. Don't be afraid to try again in six months. Ask when the best time of year is and try to schedule an appearance then.

If you want a celebrity to make a guest appearance or give a speech to your group, go ahead and make contact. While you may not be able to get the hottest star, you'll never know what luminary you can get until you try.

Recruiting Out-of-State Speakers (Without Spending a Fortune)

Have you ever wanted to have an out-of-state Christian author or artist come talk to your group but didn't have the budget to fly them in, let alone pay a large honorarium? Call your local Christian radio and television stations and ask what authors or artists they are bringing to town during the next few months. Then suggest that you would like to piggyback on their appearance and have them speak to the single adult group, should their schedules allow. Our singles group has done this several times with authors, and it allowed the group to meet some writers whose books they have read over the years.

Since the celebrity's expenses are met by the station, publisher, or record label, your only obligation may be an honorarium. Some Christian authors and artists reduce or eliminate their normal fee under these circumstances because this is free advertising for them.

Proper Care of Guest Speakers

Booking Guest Speakers. When booking guest speakers, there are a number of questions to ask and details to cover to insure that both parties know what is expected of them and to make the speaker's time with you pleasant and productive. Here are a few items the host group must discuss with the speaker.

When trying to book a guest speaker for your group, you should raise the issue of the honorarium. If you can give one, mention the amount and do not keep the speaker guessing how much it will be.

Ask whether the speaker needs any equipment other than a podium and microphone. Some may need a slide or film projector, a VCR, or a chalkboard.

Immediately following the speaker's acceptance, send a follow-up letter to the speaker outlining the details of the event, the time frame for the talk, and the agreed upon honorarium or a word of thanks for the gratis talk. If your street address is difficult to find, include a map to your building showing the best parking lot and the easiest entrance. If the speaker anticipates a late arrival, reserve a parking space for him or her.

Have an attendant present to bring the speaker directly to the meeting room upon arrival.

It is often wise to call the speaker a day before the scheduled appearance as a reminder of the event. Thank the speaker again for coming and review the equipment needs, time frame, transportation, and whatever other issues may be important. Treat this person with courtesy and consideration, just as you would want to be treated.

For a speaker flying in from out of town, find out the flight number and arrival time, and be there early to meet him or her. If you and the speaker do not know each other, you should wear a name tag to the airport. Or have a small sign with either your name or the group name on it. Make sure other arrangements are final before the speaker arrives. The host arranges for lodging, meals, car rental, or other transportation to and from the event.

Proper introductions. Being a speaker and often a master of ceremonies myself, I have been on both ends of introductions. I cannot emphasize enough the importance of proper introductions.

The purpose of an introduction is not to inflate the ego of the speaker with a lot of glowing remarks about his or her accomplishments. Rather, the main purpose of a good introduction is to assure the audience that the speaker has the credentials to present his or her speech. A good introduction bridges the gap between an unknown speaker and the audience. Mention the speaker's educational background, professional credits, and any other information, even personal achievements, that encourage the audience to listen.

Never, never introduce a speaker like this:

> I have never met the speaker before, but I was handed this paper with some information on it. It looks like he has done a lot, but I won't bore you with his accomplish-

ments. So here he is, our speaker for the evening—John Doe.

Or,

We are glad to have Mary Smith to talk to us tonight. I know she has done a lot of things, but if she wants you to know about them, I will let her tell you. Here she is—Mary Smith.

Be aware of the importance of setting the stage for the speaker. Any speaker deserves at least a few kind words in a well-spoken, proper introduction.

Gracious closures. A good closure is just as important as a good introduction. Listen carefully to the talk and use something that was said in thanking the speaker publicly for his talk. After the applause, the master of ceremonies should make a few, brief, positive comments about the talk and say something like, "I'm glad I came tonight to hear this excellent presentation. I learned a lot about (the topic). Thanks again, Mr. Jones." Another way of concluding is to mention something that was said, then say something a bit more personal—"I'm glad this man is in charge of (then mention his area of responsibility). With him in charge, I have every confidence that their clients/customers will be treated fairly." If the audience liked his presentation, they will give him another round of applause. The first applause is an obligation of the audience; it says the audience is glad he came. The second applause, if done right, will make the speaker glad *he* came.

Other things to remember. Place a glass of cool water on the podium and bring another glass of water or refreshment to the speaker after the talk. If the crowd presses for handshakes and personal introductions, the speaker will not have the time to get anything to eat or drink. Don't make him or her endure "dry mouth" or have to ask for help. Anticipate any typical needs you can.

Give the speaker a check that day for services agreed upon and rendered. If he or she incurred other expenses, send a check within the week.

For a touch of class, send the speaker a thank you card and say something nice and personal about her or his speech. If the speaker did a good job, tell her or him so after the meeting and also put it in writing in your thank you note.

How to Help Your Speaker Bomb!

Here are a few tongue-in-cheek suggestions to help your speaker have a horrible time and ruin the program.

1. Leave messages requesting him or her to speak, but never leave a phone number, a date, the topic, or the name of your organization.
2. When discussing the engagement, don't say anything about an honorarium. Make the speaker sweat it out or ask.
3. After booking the speaker, don't send any follow-up information, and don't stay in touch with him or her regarding the details.
4. Don't help with travel arrangements or meet the speaker at the airport.
5. Don't make lodging arrangements; the speaker is sure to enjoy driving around and seeing the sights after an exhausting flight.
6. Don't make any meal arrangements; the speaker will have plenty of time to drive around in a strange city looking for good restaurants.
7. Don't have the meeting room set up in accordance with the speaker's instructions.
8. Give a poor introduction. Be sure to mispronounce the speaker's name. When the

talk is over, go directly to the next item on the
agenda without acknowledging the speech or
speaker.

9. Never send the speaker a thank you note.

10. Forget to give the speaker the check. Wait a
couple of months, and then send it without apology.

Networking with Other Groups

Singles groups, especially small ones, benefit from
doing joint activities with other singles groups. There
are two ways to network: among churches within your
own denomination, locally and regionally; and with
other singles groups in your town or county. Contact
various singles leaders in other churches and groups
and invite them to a brainstorming meeting to determine whether it's possible to do joint activities and if all
parties would like to.

A variety of activities and programs can be successful
joint ventures. Co-ed sports leagues for volleyball,
softball, or bowling are wonderful activities to develop
into joint programs. Monthly meetings with other
groups for fellowship also works well. It's often a lot
more fun to go on retreats, canoe trips, and sightseeing
trips with members of other singles groups.

A number of towns across the country have singles
associations. Three examples of such associations follow. Your single adult ministry may want to organize a
singles association in your area.

Positive Christian Singles Network of South Georgia and North Florida

Positive Christian Singles is a network of about 900
South Georgia and North Florida single adults of all
ages who attend one of many different churches.

PCS's purpose is to provide single persons with the
opportunity to make new friends and to participate in

dialogue, fun, fellowship, and personal growth by sponsoring dances, parties, trips, sports, outdoor activities, various support groups, Bible studies, spiritual discussions, and going out together. Children are welcome at most activities.

PCS is a nonprofit, self-supporting organization with no dues. It relies on volunteers, contributions, fundraising events, and ads in the monthly newsletter for financial support.

Christian Singles Fellowship of Huntsville

In Huntsville, Alabama, single church members joined forces to offer special programs to single adults throughout the city. Christian Singles Fellowship, Inc., includes Presbyterian, Roman Catholic, Southern Baptist, Episcopal, Christian Church (Disciples of Christ), United Methodist, Lutheran, and independent churches.

CSF sponsors major gatherings such as an open Christmas dinner and celebration, ice cream socials, and group excursions to interesting places. Additionally, CSF has compiled a Directory of Christian Singles Groups for the area.

As a result of CSF's activities, singles in the community have Christian alternatives for recreation, and participating groups draw support and ideas from one another for their respective churches.

A Mid-Illinois Group

Some thirty-three Christian singles groups in and around the Peoria area recently came together for a two-day enrichment conference. They plan to reach out to forty-two counties in central Illinois and regularly bring together single adults from all denominations for a Christian sharing experience. Local pastors have been very supportive and helpful.

LEARN FROM PROGRAM EVALUATIONS

After any special program that the group wants to repeat some time in the future, you should analyze or evaluate the program from all angles. Record the positive as well as the negative aspects of the event. Such evaluations are critical to the success of the program the next time you plan this event or one similar to it.

For example, a few years ago our singles group planned and produced our annual ice cream concert, which usually attracts single adults from all over the greater Kansas City area. In making plans for this same annual event the following year, I opened my files and referred to my evaluation notes of last year's program. Those notes reminded me of certain things that needed to be changed as well as successful elements that should be repeated. I read in my notes that the platform area the band used last year became too hot. We needed to supply more fans to cool and ventilate the platform area for the benefit of the five musicians. So, this year we brought in several more fans for the band. They were much more comfortable.

As I continued reading my evaluation from last year, I noticed that we purchased too much ice cream and toppings. This year we purchased less. The result was that we accurately predicted the consumption of ice cream and saved money by not buying so much.

Involve officers and other key singles in the evaluation process. They probably noticed something you didn't. Do the evaluation soon after the event while the details are still fresh in everyone's mind. File away the evaluation until next year.

Use the Activity Evaluation Form on the following page to evaluate each activity, program or event. Remember to file each form for future reference.

ACTIVITY EVALUATION FORM

Name of activity: _____

Number of people attending: _____

PIC _____

How was this activity publicized/promoted? newsletter; advertise-ment(s); press release; brochure(s); special hand-outs; verbal an-nouncements in group meeting and/or church.

Briefly evaluate the effectiveness of the publicity/promotion: _____
_____

What can be done to increase attendance next time? _____
_____
_____

What outside factors may have had an impact on this activity
(weather, competing events, time of year, etc.)? _____
_____
_____

List two things participants enjoyed most about this activity: _____

1. _____
2. _____

What parts of the activity need improvement next time? _____
_____

Was this activity successful enough to repeat at a future date?

   Yes   No

If not, why not? _____

Final Thoughts on Developing Programs

Working with Singles of All Ages in the Same Group

Many small groups contain single adults of all ages, young and old. One of the questions I often hear at leadership seminars is "How do I work effectively with people representing a wide range of ages in the same group?" Here are a few suggestions.

Alternate programs and activities so there is something for everyone over a period of time. Younger singles are usually more interested in career, love, dating, sex, and marriage issues. They tend to be more energetic and enjoy active games and programs.

Older singles are often more interested in programs concerning financial security, retirement, health issues, and remarriage. The activities they like are those that are less strenuous and more sedentary like movies, cards, or table games. They are often interested in history and appreciate museum trips.

Do keep in mind that there are exceptions to the above. Some young people are vitally interested in planning for their financial security, and some older persons have a keen interest in relationship or career issues.

Generally speaking, middle-aged singles are the most flexible when adapting to programs targeted to other age groups. Some middle singles will identify with the younger group, while others will enjoy the programs aimed at the older single.

Here's one program idea you can do with a group that contains single adults of all ages: Divide your group into different age groups, and have each group discuss a single question or topic as it relates to their group. Or you could assign different topics to the groups. The small groups then return to the larger session for final thoughts and a wrap-up.

You may be thinking, "But our class isn't big enough to split into age groups. We would only have three people in some groups!" While it is difficult to have single adults of all ages in the same small group, it's best to have one small group of mixed ages than to have several tiny groups with only three to five people in each. One of the axioms in working with single adults is "The larger the group, the better."

Generally speaking, if your group has a wide range of ages, plan most programs and activities with the middle-aged group in mind.

Programming for Older Single Men and Women

If current trends continue, half of all women entering their senior years will be single. According to the Journal of Gerontology, "While it seems to have stabilized among people under forty, the divorce rate for women over forty is on the increase."[1] What is your church doing for the large numbers of older women who are becoming single again? These women have wisdom and maturity that can enrich your group. Help them make new friends and use their leadership skills to further develop your group. Many of them will enjoy training younger people in the singles ministry. Give them an opportunity to re-establish their identity and affirm their value. Most of all they need a place to be themselves.

Older single women aren't the only ones who need a little extra attention: Statistics indicate that single men die earlier than married men. It is important for singles groups to include middle-aged and older single men in their activities. Many men have fewer coping skills than women and need more support systems to help them survive the stress and trauma of single life. One suggestion is to establish a senior adult program that brings men and women together. Home parties, dinners, movies, table games, and nonathletic group activities suit both sexes in a senior adult program.

For additional social outlets, refer older adults to other senior adult programs in your community.

Daytime Single Adult Ministry

Some singles groups are large enough to offer programs and activities during the daytime. These programs are organized around a breakfast or lunch for those who work nights or are unable to attend an evening program.

Ambassadors for Christ, at the College Hill Presbyterian Church in Cincinnati, started a morning group. They met from 10:30 A.M. to 12:30 P.M. for Bible study and discussion. Six or seven people attended the first morning meeting.

Terry Fisher, the Ambassadors leader at that time, told me that all the people who attend worked strange hours. One was a pilot with a varied schedule, another was a youth worker who spent many of his evenings with teenagers, and others were self-employed and used that study as a good break from work. Terry also said that they planned social activities in the afternoons because many things, such as movies and plays, are cheaper at that time.

Consider organizing a daytime group around lunch time. Having lunch together, whether at the beginning or end of the meeting, is a meaningful time together.

Avoid Xerox Programming

Is your group doing original programming or is it merely a "Xerox ministry"? A Xerox ministry is one that simply copies what everyone else is doing without putting much thought into it.

Now, there are some universal programs a lot of us

do, like having a Sunday school for single adults or a weeknight Bible study or a support group for recently divorced people. These are good, productive activities. Do them, if they work for your single adult ministry.

But remember to leave room for creativity within your own planning and programming. Challenge the singles group to do something unique. Offer a program no one else has done. This will help keep your singles ministry fresh and vital.

Now that you have developed a healthy, interesting variety of programs for the single adults in your church or area, how do you let people know what you're doing? Let's talk about publicity.

CHAPTER **7**

▲

The Value of Good Publicity

I've often heard that if you have good programs, people will beat a path to your doorstep. This statement is only half true. People will beat a path to your door IF they know what you have to offer.

That's where good publicity comes in. If the singles group has a good program, let people know about it. In a very small town, word of mouth may be sufficient, but in larger areas it usually takes additional publicity to get the word out. Good programs deserve to be publicized. This chapter introduces various kinds of publicity to effectively promote single adult programs to your community.

KEYS TO EFFECTIVE PROMOTIONS

Start Early

Start early and take plenty of time to produce a quality product. It always takes longer than it should to complete a good promotional piece. Start early and plan on a few delays in the process.

Use the Five W's Guidline

When writing promotional copy, include all the essential facts: who, what, where, when, why—and how much!

Use Good Grammar

Always use good grammar. For help, call the grammar hotline in your area. (For a directory of local grammar hotlines, send a self-addressed, stamped envelope to Hotline Directory, Tidewater Community College Writing Center, 1700 College Crescent, Virginia Beach, Virginia 23456.)

Take Time to Proofread

Before going to press, ask someone else to proof your promotional copy. Once you've written it, you are not the best person to proof the copy. You're too familiar with it. Your proofreader should have excellent spelling and grammar and a great eye for detail. He or she will find typos, ambiguities, and misspelled words and make suggestions to improve the clarity of the message. Proofreading saves a lot of headaches and money on printing. When revisions are made, don't assume they are correct; proofread the revisions as well.

Don't Forget the Return Address

When sending out self-mailers (flyers that bear the recipient's address and consequently don't need envelopes), make certain a return address is printed in the upper left-hand corner.

Over the years, I've received numerous mailing pieces where the return address was missing. On a few occasions, the organization's name was not even mentioned inside the brochure! They assumed I knew who they were. A return address safeguards against anonymous flyers.

Another reason to include a return address is to obtain address corrections. If the label is misaddressed, the post office uses the return address to return the flyer.

If you use envelopes, beware: With the volume of mail people receive today, some people may open an envelope then discard it while saving the enclosures to read later. Once they've disposed of the envelope, they have no way of knowing how to respond unless the name and address of your ministry is on the inside material. Always put the name and return address on the material inside the envelope as well as on the envelope itself.

Create a Positive Image

Printed publicity material is sometimes the first contact the singles group has with prospective new members. The image of the group is directly related to the quality of the publicity. To create a positive image, use a good typewriter, word processor, or professional typesetter; use sharp graphics—in color, if possible. Make your message simple and friendly. Make it appealing.

Kevin McLaughlin, in his article "Running Your Business," says that the area most often overlooked when establishing a company's professional image is the quality of their written material. The business card, various brochures, and the company's other promotional literature make strong first impressions, for better or worse.

The same holds true for single adult ministries. Sloppy material gives the impression of a sloppy, unorganized group.

Send it Out on Time

Have you ever received in the mail a brochure inviting you to a program a day after the event? Send out an activities calendar well in advance of the first event. People need a certain amount of lead time before being able to make commitments. Send promotional literature a week to ten days before any deadlines or dates for the event.

Use an "Early-Bird" Incentive

Encourage people to make reservations for programs and activities early. Offer them an early-bird discount or other incentive to sign up early. Human nature, especially with singles, is to wait until the last minute before making a commitment. An early-bird incentive often motivates people to register.

Track the Results

Measure the success of promotional literature by keeping track of which approach produces the greatest response.

There are different ways to track brochures and flyers with reservation forms. Fan the brochures or flyers and run an ink mark on the edge of the reservation form. Or put marks in different locations on the brochures to indicate different ways the brochure was distributed. When the forms arrive, look for those little ink marks, and keep a tally of how many returned from various locations.

Space advertising in newspapers and magazines can be tracked by adding a different code number to each publication. Another way to track results is to ask on the visitor's form how they learned about the singles group or activity.

With the high cost of printing and advertising, find

out what kind of promotion produces the best results and use your budget for that kind of publicity.

Keep Your Artwork

Maintain a file for previously used artwork. It may be useful again and thus will save on production costs.

Proper Placement

Advertising doesn't always get the results you hope for. Effective advertising requires proper placement. If you are located in a metropolitan area, ask the advertising department of the largest newspaper whether they have any research to indicate which section of the paper is heavily read by single adults. As the buyer, you have some control over which section the ad will appear in. Often the entertainment section is a good place for an ad to reach single adults.

Ads in the largest newspaper in town offer the greatest visibility, but they also cost the most money. If you live in a suburban area, consider advertising in neighborhood newspapers. This is cheaper and pinpoints the geographical area you want to reach.

In addition to standard display ads in area newspapers, be aware of other publications with a high readership among single adults. For example, the Saturn Road Church of Christ in Garland, Texas, has promoted its singles ministry through classified ads in a large health club news magazine. The ads encouraged singles "looking for a place to belong" to join the Saturn Road Singles where they will find "significance, acceptance, wholesome relationships, or just a friend." Other churches have found it effective to advertise in local television or shopper's guides.

Remember these five tips on newspaper and magazine advertising.

1. Research the publications in your area, and keep a file on their advertising rates.
2 Ask if they have a church rate.
3. Have your ad professionally typeset (most newspapers do this as part of their service).
4. Dress it up with graphics, screens, reverses, or color.
5. Always proofread the ad layout before giving final approval for printing.

WAYS TO GET FREE PUBLICITY

News Releases

Properly written and sent, news releases bring a lot of free publicity in the form of public service announcements. Here are a few guidelines for creating good news releases.

Write a news release with the idea of a V or an inverted pyramid in mind. In other words, put your most important information in the first paragraph, the next most important in the second paragraph, and so on. Each subsequent paragraph may embellish an item in the first paragraph—but put all essential information in that first paragraph. Editors with limited space cut news releases from the bottom up and assume the most important information is at the top.

Double space the news release and keep it to one page. Put a contact person's name and phone number at the end of the release. The editor may need to clarify or confirm something in the release. Include an evening phone number because many editors work afternoon or evening shifts and may need to call after normal working hours. Also indicate at the top of the page (flush right margin) the best time for the release to run. For example: For release September 6-14. This helps the editor know the best time for his audience to know about the event. See the sample news release below.

Sample News Release:

(for release September 6-14)

DENNIS ALLEN TO SPEAK TO COUNTRYSIDE SINGLES

Dennis Allen, star of stage and TV, will be the guest speaker Sunday, September 15, for both singles classes at Oak Hill Christian Church.

Allen, a native Kansas Citian, has a long list of credits, including appearing as a regular on "The Leslie Uggams Show" and on Rowan and Martin's "Laugh-in." He has appeared in many TV specials and talk shows and has been in numerous industrial shows. He has also done more than 100 national commercials. In addition to acting, he has also written and directed many shows and plays. A favorite dinner-theater actor in Kansas City, Allen has performed in more than 20 local productions and has been the host for "All Night Live" on local TV. He also established the Performing Arts Program for emotionally disturbed children at the Arizona Boys Ranch in Phoenix, Arizona. He holds a Master of Fine Arts degree from Boston University.

All singles are cordially invited to hear Allen speak to both singles classes. The New Horizons class (for singles of all ages) starts at 9:30 A.M. and the Discovery class (for singles up to mid-30s) at 11:00.

For more information, contact Rev. Ron Andrews, Singles Minister, Oak Hill Christian Church, 6101 Greene Avenue, Mission, Kansas 66202. Telephone: 555-2520.

CAPSULE STATEMENT:
DENNIS ALLEN TO SPEAK TO OAK HILL SINGLES.

Dennis Allen, star of Laugh-in and many local dinner theater productions, will speak September 15 to both singles classes at Oak Hill Christian Church, 6101 Greene Ave., Mission, Kansas. The classes meet at 9:30 A.M. and at 11:00 A.M. The singles public is cordially invited.

(For media verification only: Andrews's home phone is 555-2921.)

Create a master mailing list of the various media—newspapers, shopper guides, magazines, radio and TV stations, and denominational publications. Each time you send a release, simply photocopy the list onto peel-off labels.

Send a copy of the news release to each appropriate editor on the mailing list. In other words, should a release be appropriate for several different sections of a large newspaper (for example, Religion, Entertainment, or Lifestyle), send a copy of the release to the editor of each section. Editors within a newspaper seldom share their releases; it is up to you to send it to each particular department for consideration.

Mail the news release two weeks before the event you wish to publicize. For monthly publications, ask about their deadlines, its usually two to four weeks before the publication date.

Finally, remember that the media has no obligation to publicize your news release. Publicity is free advertising, but don't count solely on that. Still, it's the first place to start because it has enormous potential, should the news release run. To guarantee promotion of a program, consider a form of paid advertising.

Invite Media Coverage

If the event or program is newsworthy, alert local media to the event and invite them to attend. If an editor calls to verify or clarify something in your news release, invite that editor to cover the event as a news story. Suggest they bring a photographer to take pictures. The major newspaper in my town did a story on one of our big activities and put a picture of the event in the paper. The picture filled a half page. That story and picture brought us priceless publicity.

OTHER FORMS OF PROMOTION

An Activities Newsletter

One of the key ingredients to a successful singles ministry is a good newsletter that provides details of upcoming events. Verbal announcements of activities are helpful, but it is far better to print that information and distribute it to members and potential visitors. Written information draws greater participation. Here are some guidelines for an effective newsletter.

Gather all the details.

The reader must have the basic information on each activity.

- What—Describe the event.
- Where—Tell where it will be held.
- Date—Give the day and date of the event (i.e., Saturday, February 11).
- Time—state the starting and ending time.
- Food—If food is involved, specify what to bring, what it costs, the time the meal is served.
- Cost—Specify how much the event will cost and when the fee must be paid.
- RSVP—Indicate deadlines and how to RSVP (by sign-up, phone, pre-registration, etc.).
- Kids—Announce whether children are welcome or the availability of child care.

Make It Interesting

Add interest to the newsletter by including a few of the following items.

- A list of birthdays for the month.
- Describe a "mystery person" (choose a person from the group but don't give the name—let the readers try to guess who it is).

- A list of future events.
- A short quote or anecdote.
- Other news such as wedding announcements; addresses of former members who have relocated to another city; help needed for special projects; or further elaboration of any of the items mentioned in the calendar section.
- Print a calendar with the activities noted on the appropriate days.

Type the newsletter neatly

Proofread it for typos.

Dress it up graphically

Add some clip art or pictures.

Print the newsletter using colored ink or colored stock

Make it look professionally printed (don't use duplicating machines that blur the type).

Mail it in time

If the newsletter includes a monthly calendar, distribute it at least a week before the first event listed for that month.

Newsletters often provide the first impression of a group's personality. The singles newsletter is a great recruiting tool. Do it with class!

Brochures That Work

Brochures provide pertinent information about your program. If designed properly, they can be inserted in mailings to prospective members inquiring about your program. While brochures offer general information, they cannot give specifics on who the guest speaker is next Sunday or what's happening next Saturday night at you activity; newsletters offer specifics. The advantage to the brochure is to tell prospects about the group in general and its mission.

Business Cards

Business cards (also called care cards or calling cards) are used by many singles groups across the country. Cards are distributed to members who, in turn, give them to prospects. Some cards have printing on one side only, others include a message on the reverse side. Some use a double or fold-over card. If the church address is hard to locate, consider printing a map on the reverse side. Care cards are often dressed up by adding a second color and a logo of the church or singles group. One way to use business cards is to promote a special event. Print the name, date, time, and cost of the event on the bottom of the card. The cards are convenient to carry in one's pocket and are a constant reminder of the event.

Classified Ads

Classified ads are in the section of the paper commonly referred to as the "want ads." An advantage to advertising in this section is that the ads are less expensive. Carefully select the right classified section for your ad.

Below is a famous classified ad that was so effective it resulted in a five-part series on prime-time nightly news. All ads, however, don't have to be this long to be effective. Simply provide basic information and a phone number for further details.

DIVORCED AND SEPARATED CATHOLICS!
Is your tummy in a knot over your situation?
Feel guilty at times?
Angry at—?
Angry at your Church?

Frustrated?
Mistrust the opposite sex?
If "yes" to any of those questions, you might try:
jumping off a chair (nothing higher please),
or gulping a couple of aspirins and going to bed for a month.
OR
try meeting the warm and empathetic folks waiting for you at

"Ministry to Divorced Catholics" (MDC).
No fee. No commitments. No "sign right here...."
Interested in our free newsletter that tells all?
If so, send a stamped self-addressed envelope to:
FATHER ED HOLDEN
300 Broadway
Newark, New Jersey 07104

Display Ads

Display ads are found elsewhere in the newspaper and usually consists of varying sizes of type and a graphic element. The ads are available in many sizes and even small ones can draw attention if properly placed.

For larger sizes, have the ad professionally created to your design. Most newspapers will "build" the ad for you as part of the fee to run the ad. Always proofread the final copy before it goes to press.

Display ads are a great way to publicize something special. Ad space in neighborhood shopping guides and newspapers are fairly inexpensive.

Stock Ads

Another type of a display ad is to buy a stock ad and strip in particular information. One source for stock ads is the Church Ad Project which produces bold, provocative ads to bring people back to Christ and the church.[1] Many of the ads try to reach those who feel that the Church is ready to condemn them for leaving. Several of these ads are designed to attract singles. Some ads for singles are captioned: "You can't meet God's gift to men in a singles bar"; "If you think the church is only for families, remember that Jesus was single"; and "Contrary to popular belief, God welcomes singles too." All have appropriate graphics.

Coupons

Some churches and singles groups use innovative coupons to promote an event or to increase attendance. The First Baptist Church in downtown Denver scored a big success by implementing an old-fashioned grocery-store technique to bolster church attendance—passing out coupons. First-time visitors to the church receive a coupon or gift book that entitles them to a free lunch on Tuesdays, free one-day parking in the church's prime downtown parking lot, and two reserved seats in the front pew.

Now doesn't that start creative juices flowing with ideas for coupons to give away in your singles group to promote attendance? Print coupons that would entitle the user to a free admission at the next social event; a free lunch with the Lunch Bunch; or a free ticket to the Valentine Banquet. Have fun with this idea! The following coupons may be duplicated or adapted to fit programs for the single adult ministry in your church. The sample Visitor Coupon invites visitors to a lunch after church—this makes visitors feel special and offers members of the single adult ministry the opportunity to meet new people over lunch. The sample You Are A Winner coupon can be adapted for any activity, event, or program. Remember to add the name, address, and phone number of your church on the bottom of every coupon you create.

▲
VISITOR COUPON

Name:_____

As a first-time visitor to our singles group, you are invited to be our guest for a Sunday luncheon.

Please join our "Lunch Bunch" and hand this coupon to one of the officers or "regulars" at lunch. You will be reimbursed for your meal (up to $5.00).

Coupon must be redeemed by: (date) _____

There is always a warm welcome for all singles at: (your church name) _____

▲

YOU ARE A WINNER!

Name:_____

Congratulations! You have won an activity of your choice sponsored by our singles group.

Please choose from the list of activities printed in the newsletter.

Redeem this coupon at the next singles meeting for reimbursement ($5.00 maximum).

Coupon must be redeemed by: (date) _____

 All singles have a home at: (your church name) _____

Directory of Singles Groups

Contribute to a directory of singles groups in your area. These directories are often listings of groups in local newspapers or local singles magazines. Sometimes the directory is a separate publication that lists and describes all the singles groups in the area. Usually there is no charge to be listed. Call the publisher or editor to be included in the next listing. Ask whether there is a fee and when the next deadline is.

Apartment Newsletters

Some groups have had successful results running an ad or article in various apartment newsletters. Target complexes with a large number of single adult residents.

Community College Seminars

If your church happens to be located in a town large enough to have a community college, contact the community education director and suggest that you offer seminars dealing with singles issues. Offer a session for singles interested in the various singles groups and activities available in your city. Or offer a series on grief or divorce recovery through the community college.

There are a couple of advantages to offering seminars through the college. The college handles all promotion and registration for the course. And their publicity usually reaches far more singles than the church and attracts singles who might not otherwise respond to a church promotion.

Also offer these seminars in your church, not just at the college. Seminars at the church subtly introduce your church to those who attend and makes it easier for them to return in the future for another activity.[2]

Scoreboard Recognition

At athletic events, ask how many tickets you need to buy to have the singles group name listed on the scoreboard as a visiting group. Even if you can't sell all the tickets required to be listed, consider buying them anyway because of the large number of people who will see your group name listed on the scoreboard.

Write Articles for Local Papers

If someone in the singles group is a talented writer,

ask about various issues concerning single activities for your local newspaper or singles magazine. Most publications give the writer and group a byline.

Handouts, Flyers, and Posters

Handouts and flyers are often posted in such places as grocery stores, laundromats, variety and drug stores. Don't overlook this kind of publicity when promoting a special event. Some places, such as libraries, will even allow you to leave a stack of flyers for people to pick up.

If you put up posters for a certain event, be sure to retrace your steps after the event is over and take them down. When you remove old posters, most businesses will let you post something again in the future.

A Unique Logo

Ask artistically gifted singles in the group to create a logo for the group. Use the logo on letterhead, business cards, in your ads, and other promotional literature.

Direct Mail

Direct mail is often a successful way to reach singles—if you have a good mailing list. If you don't have such a mailing list, rent a mailing list from a commercial list broker in your area. List brokers help you locate a list predominantly composed of single adults. You'll have to pay a fee for the list, but direct mail can pay dividends. Average response to direct mail is about 1 to 3 percent. To explore direct mail as a promotional vehicle, contact a local direct-mail company for advice regarding beginning a direct-mail program.

Word of mouth

"A satisfied customer is the best advertising." But remember, this may be the most powerful publicity, but it's also the slowest.

Piggybacking

Piggybacking is riding along with or hooking onto another event or program. When advertising one particular event, piggyback it with another activity as well. Piggybacking saves money. For example, in preparing a brochure to promote a big singles dance, use the back side to promote a divorce recovery workshop or a special speaker in the Sunday school class.

Not all occasions readily allow for piggybacking, but be aware of opportunities.

Other clever ideas

Keep thinking of new ways to publicize the single adult ministry. Here are three ideas that attracted a lot of attention.

Roses for singles. Many churches have the tradition of placing roses on the pulpit to signify the birth of new babies into the congregation. But the Countryside Christian Church in suburban Kansas City recently shocked its congregation one Sunday by having twenty-two roses on the pulpit. Each rose symbolized twenty-two persons who attended the brand-new singles Sunday school class the church had started the previous week.

Getting the front cover. Buy the front cover of your local TV schedule to promote your singles group. That's just what the First United Methodist Church of Carrollton, Texas, did to publicize their Positive Christian Singles group. That television schedule claimed to have 30,000 readers in the northwestern suburbs of Dallas where Carrollton is located.

"Here comes the judge." The copy below appeared on a card to describe one group in Decatur, Alabama. It is attached to each divorce decree granted by the local judge.

This same card is also printed on day-glo stock sent

to all newcomers in town. The singles ministry works with the Welcome Wagon to locate new singles.

SAVE THIS CARD

You may not need it right now, but the SINGLES AND SINGLES AGAIN CLASS may be just the place for you.
We offer to Single Adults: a family to share life with you, coffee and discussion on Sunday morning, a Sunday lunch bunch, Wednesday dinners, Divorce and Grief Recovery Groups, cook-outs and parties almost every weekend, and wonderful friendships. We work really hard at keeping S & SA as a support group and from being just one more dating situation.

If you want to find out more about this group of over 300 enrolled singles, then call Sally Booth at 555-4792, or Asa Sparks at 555-2730, or the church office at 555-6941.

We will tell you where the next Wednesday dinner will be (children are welcome), or you can just show up Sunday at Central United Methodist Church, 616 Jackson St., SE, Decatur, at 9:00 A.M. Come in the front door of the second building on Jackson St., turn left, open the fire door and come to the second floor, walk to the other end of the hall where all the happiness can be heard.

Publicity opportunities are limited only by the collective imagination of the entire single adult ministry. Plan occasional publicity brainstorming sessions with interested members of the singles group to get the creative juices flowing. Imaginative, creative publicity is guaranteed to reach singles in your church and community.

CHAPTER 8

▲

The Matter of Money

This chapter looks at a number of issues concerning money. These issues range from making your activities self-supporting to subsidizing activities for the children; from "love loans" to scholarships; and from creative ways of financing single adult ministry to the use of early-bird deadlines.

SOURCES OF FUNDING

One of the questions often asked by churches wanting to start a single adult ministry is "How does a church finance such a program?"

Most singles programs are financed directly through the church budget. This is the most common way of supporting church programs, including a single adult ministry.

If the general church budget is the source of money for the singles ministry, expenses must be calculated in advance and entered into the budget. Apart from staff salary, the other single adult ministry expenses budgeted are: the staff automobile and activity expenses (so the staff person can attend outside events with the group without its draining his or her salary); program expenses for special speakers; advertising and promotional expenses; publication expenses; conference and seminar fees; plus any ordinary office expenses. In most cases, annual budgets are submitted to the congregation for approval.

Activity Fees

Most singles events and activities should be self-sustaining. The church budget must not be expected to pay for the social activities of single adults any more than it would pay for the social activities of any other group within the church. With rare exceptions, such as with outreach programs, activities should pay for themselves.

Most singles activities require money. Determine the cost of the event and charge attendees an appropriate fee so the event will be self-supporting. However, consider subsidizing the price of children's tickets to family activities so single parents can bring their children without its being a financial hardship.

Registration and Payments

Occasionally, an activity requires advance reservations to properly plan for the event. Some people will make reservations but not show up for the activity. To eliminate no-shows for events with firm reservations, require advance payment when people make their reservations. In other words, their payment becomes their reservation. Requiring advance payment means giving plenty of advance notice on the details of the event, the cost, and the deadline for reservations.

A technique to get people to pay early for annual activities such as canoe trips or retreats is the early-bird discount, which requires payment one or two weeks before the deadline in exchange for a discount on the cost of the activity. Singles save a little money by paying early and also help the planners for the event know about how many people will attend.

Offerings and Fundraisers

Many churches, especially those with single adult Sunday school classes, collect regular offerings and conduct fundraisers for the ministry. Offerings may be collected weekly or only when a special need comes to the attention of the group.

Fundraisers are another way to raise support for a singles program or special event. Sometimes substantial sums can be raised. Many organizations in the nation rely heavily upon fundraisers as their major means of support.

While some churches do not believe in the philosophy behind fundraising, it nevertheless has an advantage apart from the money that is raised. Fundraising often creates camaraderie among those participating in the activity. (For more information, see Ch. 15, "Fundraising.")

Keep offerings and monies from fundraisers in a separate account from the one administered through the church budget. The singles minister or leader handles funds provided by the general church budget and is responsible for the expenditure of those funds. The single adult group or class administers a separate account created by offerings and fundraising. The officers decide how to spend this money. The treasurer keeps records of where the money comes from and where it goes. Should the ministry leader run out of budget money for the group or have a special project requiring extra money, he or she may negotiate with the officers of the singles group for a transfer of funds. Generally, the singles group account is an in-and-out account for deposits (of activity tickets sold, for example) and withdrawals (to pay for those tickets).

Corporate Grants

Some churches secure special monies for their

programs by seeking grants from large corporations or foundations. Unless you already know of possible grants (such as key business persons in the congregation), contact the various corporations and foundations in your city and discover which ones donate money to church programs.

Most grants require a written proposal, which includes objectives, budget, and future funding. Also, many foundations only consider funding proposals a couple of times a year—so be prepared to submit the proposal many months before starting your program.

As is true with so many things, getting a grant is often a matter of knowing the right people. Search your congregation for people connected to grant sources and work through them. If you have a valid grant proposal prepared, don't be afraid to use whatever contacts you can to get consideration.

Special Donations

Some funds may come in the form of a special gift. Someone in your congregation may wish to donate money for a single adult ministry. Some may make a donation because they know the value of a good singles group to their church. Others who have been widowed or divorced themselves or have a divorced son or daughter may choose to donate money. Make an appeal to anyone interested in establishing a singles ministry to donate to the cause.

If you already have a group organized but need money for a specific use, invite people to give to that specific need. For example, some may donate money to buy a new desk or to renovate an office for the singles minister. Others may contribute to a sinking fund for a large event the group wants to do. Others may give money to finance an advertising campaign or a mass mailing to publicize a special singles event. However, be careful not to ask for money from people all the time.

GOOD USES FOR YOUR MONEY

Scholarships

Some single adults may want to attend major events but simply don't have the money to do so. Offer a few scholarships to those who wish to attend but can't because they lack the money. Planners of the event may reserve a few "giveaway" tickets for those who can't afford a to buy one. Or work with the ticketing agency to obtain a few complimentary tickets. When awarding scholarships or free tickets, make the offer confidential so as not to embarrass the recipient.

Don't let money be a factor in keeping people from attending singles events. Keep costs and prices down, and provide scholarships whenever possible.

Emergency Fund

From time to time, some single individuals may need emergency financial help to see them through a few weeks or months. Since the church is not a savings and loan institution, most churches do not plan financial assistance into their budget. However, one way to offer a very practical service to single adults is to create an emergency fund for those in need of short-term help.

The emergency fund is administrated by a small committee of people, the singles leader and one or two others, including the treasurer. When a single adult needs an emergency loan (due to suddenly losing a job, health emergencies, etc.), the committee meets to decide whether the need is legitimate and funds are sufficient to meet the need. Then the committee issues a check and requests a promise from the person in need to repay the money by a certain date. Do not charge interest if the money is repaid.

How do you create such a fund? One group started an emergency fund when a former member donated part of her inheritance to the single adult ministry. Another group started a fund when several people realized fellow members sometimes needed help—they donated the money to start it. From time to time, announce that an emergency fund exists and invite people to use it if they need to or to donate to it if they are able.

Encourage the emergency fund committee to use discernment regarding individual requests for loans. Develop general guidelines about the kinds of emergencies that qualify. But don't be too harsh or strict; the purpose is to help, not hinder, those in need.

Group Donations

When the single adult ministry is blessed with extra money in its treasury, consider donating some of the extra money to a worthwhile project or charity. You could donate the money to:

- Someone in the group with a special financial need.
- A poor family at Thanksgiving or Christmas.
- A local or national charity.
- A children's home or a home for battered women.
- The church building fund in the name of the singles group.
- A home for retired missionaries.
- A fund for sending flowers to any member who is hospitalized or has had a death in their family.
- A gift to those in the singles group who get married.

There are always people in need and many ways extra money can be used for ministry. Give money away joyfully, for it is still "more blessed to give than to receive."

CHAPTER 9

▲

General Administrative Tips and Suggestions

This chapter offers a number of ideas, insights, and suggestions for enhancing single adult ministry. Ideas range from the physical layout of the room to ways you can save time on the job. Read them all. Use those suggestions that best serve the needs of the singles ministry in your church.

ROOM DYNAMICS

Give Your Meeting Room a Warm Personality

Have you ever been in someone's home where you were not allowed to drink or eat in any room except the dining room or kitchen? A home where everything was sparkling clean and always in place? If so, you were probably a little tense and not very comfortable. While warm people help produce a relaxed atmosphere, the personality of the room itself must also be considered.

For example, some homes have a room for formal gatherings and a family room for relaxing and lounging around. Most people prefer the family room where they can kick off their shoes, have a snack, and enjoy each other's company. This is the room that contains the warmth.

Churches also have both kinds of rooms. The sanctuary is the formal room, a separate and special place where we worship God corporately. But what about the rest of the church? Is it filled with more formal rooms, or does it have lots of family rooms? More specifically, what image does the singles room present? Does it offer people a warm and friendly atmosphere, or is it rather sterile and starchy, like the formal rooms in some homes?

Here are a few things that create a sense of warmth in a room: a rug and drapes; a coffee pot and table; soft chairs; lamps rather than over headlights; and walls covered with wallpaper or paneling instead of just paint. A warm color scheme is also very important as are seasonal decorations, which help to give the room freshness and a change of pace.

Take a careful look at the room where single adults hold their meetings. Is it one that invites people to enter and relax? Or is it one that says, "Only the clean may enter—and don't mess up anything." Remember, it's much easier to build a sense of community when the meeting room is a warm, pleasant, and comfortable place that says, "Please come in and enjoy."

Take Charge of the Physical Equipment

Though it is a mundane job, the staff person or singles leader must arrive early before meetings to check out such things as chair arrangement, the sound system, air conditioning, lighting, and visual aids. Should problems with equipment arise during the meeting itself, quickly remedy the situation.

GROUP DYNAMICS

Open with Affirmation

One of the more practical things I learned in my seminary days was that one handshake before the worship service was worth two afterward. In other words, the best time to greet people is at the beginning of a service or meeting rather than at the end. An early greeting makes people feel welcome so they can enjoy what follows.

Another way to set people at ease is to offer a verbal affirmation from the podium at the very beginning of the meeting. It needn't be a long speech—just a short, warm greeting, like "Hello, it's good to see you all. This is our time together as single adults, and we're glad you are here to share this time with us. You are always welcome." When appropriate, add, "Our church (or singles ministry) is here for you seven days a week. If you ever need us, just call. We'll be happy to set aside some time to talk with you whenever you need a listening ear or a friend's advice."

Verbal affirmations are not only for regular members, but are a very important way to welcome visitors, who are usually a bit apprehensive about going to a new group. This may be the first time many visitors attend a singles event, and they really need to hear they are welcome.

Leave Some Things Unorganized

Most single adult groups are fairly well organized with officers and various committees. And it's important to have both to insure a smoothly functioning, ongoing program. But consider leaving a few things unorganized. For example, in our group, we have coffee and doughnuts before each of our Sunday school classes. Our Sunday school is fairly well organized, with a number of people having responsibilities on Sunday morning. But we purposefully leave a couple of things a little vague.

We do not assign anyone to prepare the coffee and orange juice before class. There are a few people who usually like to come early and do this. Neither do we assign specific people to help clean up when class is over. Although we divide the cleaning chores by the alphabet, we do not ask specific individuals to help—only those with last names that fall within that part of the alphabet clean up that week.

One of the reasons for not assigning people to help prepare the coffee and orange juice or help clean up is to give people the freedom to take on responsibility for their group. And becoming involved in this way helps some people to feel included. Preparing the coffee and orange juice gives them something to do and provides them with an opportunity to get involved. It's another way of feeling accepted.

From time to time very talented potential leaders come into the group, single adults who want to get involved. But if all the elected positions are taken and all the committee slots filled, they may move on to another group because they cannot find anything to do that will give them a sense of ownership and belonging. So leave a few details open-ended for those folks. It will give interested newcomers room to get planted in your group.

Use Ice-Breakers

Ice-breakers create a comfortable and relaxed atmosphere especially among people who don't know each other. Another use for ice-breakers is to stall for time when waiting for a speaker to arrive. Here are a few sample ice-breakers to get the group talking. Break the group into pairs and have each person take turns completing these sentences:

- The funniest person I ever knew was . . . .
- A faraway place I'd like to wake up in . . . .
- Two things important to me about God are . . . .
- The most fascinating business to be in is . . . .

- What I would do vocationally if I had the proper training is . . . .
- Apart from my parents, my closest relatives growing up were . . . .
- The domestic tasks I like (hate) to do the most are . . . .

Examine Your Smoking Policy

In spite of the fact that the hazards of smoking are clearly known, many continue to indulge in this habit. While most churches don't allow smoking in the building, examine your church's policy about smoking at a singles activity held in a private home or other public place.

Whether or not to allow smoking at singles events away from the church building may be a tough issue because some of the singles officers and leaders may be smokers. If the smokers go outdoors to smoke, there may not be a problem. However, one way to lose some members is to do nothing about smoking indoors with poor ventilation. Some visitors may have a low tolerance for smoke and if it is allowed, they simply may not return. Or they may tolerate it, but would rather not.

With more and more nonsmokers in the world, a number of nonsmoking singles groups have sprung up across the country. Apparently, many single adults are voicing their desire for smoke-free activities. While recognizing that many people continue to smoke, also recognize the rights of nonsmokers to enjoy an activity without having to endure a smoke-filled room. If your group passively allows smoking at events away from the church building, re-examine your smoking policy.

Be sensitive in dealing with this issue. You don't want to unnecessarily offend the smokers in the group. Some of them may be loyal, active members. Try not to lay any guilt trips on them; most know it's a bad habit and wish they could quit. Let them know that you appreciate them, but not the smoke. It's the smoke you want to eliminate, not the people. And if you deal with this gently and tactfully, most smokers will understand and comply.

As a follow-up to examining your church's smoking policy, consider a support group for single persons who really want to quit smoking. Perhaps a new policy will motivate some to kick the habit.

Pin-Point the Location

For groups that plan activities away from church, here are a few ways to help people find the activity. Create a small fabric flag with your group's initials on it. When the group goes out to a large, crowded public place—such as an outdoor concert where people sit on the grass—hoist the flag so members can spot it and find you. If you don't have flags, substitute balloons instead. Inflate them and tie them together with string (and tie several to a tall stick if you don't have helium), mark your groups initials on them, and let the balloons identify your location.

If members plan to drive themselves to an out-of-the-way event, here's a way to get them there. Print your group's initials on bright card stock (8 1/2 X 11). Position arrows on the signs. Then post the signs along the route or near the destination to help point the way to your event. In the event of rain, cover the sign with clear plastic wrap. This technique improves attendance at events because members are confident they will be able to locate unfamiliar addresses.

SERVICES YOU CAN OFFER

Moving Service

If your church owns or has access to vans and trucks,

a great way to minister to members and prospects is to help them when they move into a new home. Group members can provide strong backs to carry boxes and furniture. This can even be fun! Allow members to minister to each other.

Free Magazines

If your church or association of churches is planning a singles conference, ask about receiving free back issues of *Christian Single*. This magazine is published by the Southern Baptist Convention and is a nice item to give away at an outreach activity.

To request copies, indicate the specific number and the date you need them. Allow three weeks for delivery. Also, be sure to include your name and street address (not post office number) and phone number. Send your request to: *Christian Single*, MSN 140, 127 Ninth Avenue North, Nashville, Tennessee 37234. Please do not call.

Recorded Calendar of Events

If you are inundated with phone calls asking about weekly activities, consider putting that information on tape and letting an answering machine handle those calls. If your church is small, put all the singles activities for the month on the tape. Larger programs with lots of activities may require weekly tape changes. Publicize this activity hotline constantly so single adults will use it. And get the hotline number listed in the Yellow Pages under Singles Organizations.

Callers may also leave messages and suggestions for future group activities. Callers leave their suggestions after hearing the announcements and the beep. This is a great way to encourage suggestions from new members and others who aren't usually part of the planning process.

Exchange Table for Books and Magazines

Set up an exchange table in the singles meeting room. Invite people to donate books and magazines to the exchange table. This enables members short on money to read new material.

Place the table so it is visible and accessible. Encourage members to donate the items they ordinarily discard. Permit anyone to take from the table, even though they may not have donated a book or magazine. Announce the exchange table in the newsletter. If others use the room during the week, store the publications in a box between meetings.

RECORDS AND "HOUSEKEEPING"

A Great Use for the Video Camera

With video cameras becoming less expensive to own or rent, use them to record various activities within the singles group. Record serious meetings as well as fun activities. Assign someone who attends most activities the task of recording each important event. Try to catch the "unguarded" moments of fun and camaraderie as often as possible. If you have multiple singles groups, use separate tapes for each group.

Videotaping activities is a great way to preserve the history of the single adult ministry. Video records help members remember those who used to be in their group. The tapes may be sent to former members or to a current member who is incapacitated or hospitalized. Plan a New Year's Eve party and show a tape of "The Year in Review."

A "Master Forms" File

You'll probably find it useful to keep a file of various forms the ministry uses often. Master forms include attendance records, visitor's registration sheets, activity suggestion forms, and other forms in this book.

Exit Interviews

A relatively new trend in the business world is to invite employees leaving the company for other employment to do exit interviews. During the exit interview, former employees voice their candid thoughts on the boss, the ownership, company policies, or coworkers without fear because they have already resigned.

If the singles group is losing members, ask those who have left to give you their honest reasons for leaving. Such exit interviews often contain important clues about the group's loss of members. With that information the group can begin to solve the problems.

Keep a Log

Keep a written log of major phone calls and meetings. Record certain bits of information such as prices, policies, contact persons, and agreements that are made. As the days roll by, this log serves as a vital reference, reminding you of the details of conversations. If there is a dispute, refer to the log for clarification. Our memories sometimes play tricks on us. Keep complete minutes of your meetings too. You may forget specific decisions that were made. A record may come in handy.

Loaner Vehicles

Your ministry may need a large vehicle for trips and outings occasionally. On long trips, your single adults may not want to put extra mileage on their own cars, or they may prefer to travel in the same vehicle with their friends.

Some churches are fortunate enough to own vans and buses that can be used by the single adult ministry. But many churches have to figure out ways to get the use of a van absolutely free.

If you happen to live near an automotive assembly plant, contact their operations or public relations office about their loan policy. Some manufacturers make new vans and trucks available to nonprofit groups. Or you could advertise in the church bulletin that any "gently used" vans and trucks would be a welcome donation to the singles group.

Exchange Single Adult Newsletters

To keep up on what other singles groups are doing, offer to exchange newsletters with them. Contact their directors or leaders and invite a mutual swap. Most leaders readily agree. Swapping newsletters opens up new resources, speakers, and activity ideas.

Local singles newsletters keep you informed of what groups are doing in your area. But don't swap simply to steal other groups' program and activity ideas. If you see something in another newsletter your group would like to do, wait a while and then change it enough so that you aren't just duplicating what they have done. The exception to this are standard programs that other groups already do regularly, like talent shows, support groups, and New Year's Eve parties. Allow other local groups to keep their unique and special ideas as well as their logos and creative slogans. If you start stealing ideas, you'll stop receiving newsletters.

However, when swapping newsletters with groups across the country, it is usually all right to use their program and activity ideas since they are not competing in the same "market area" for single adults. But still be careful about using another group's logo. Let other logos be inspiration for your group to create their own.

CHAPTER **10**

▲

Visitors, Absentees, and Alumni

Trying to break into a new group is probably one of the hardest things to do. It ranks right up there with going on your first date or jumping off the high dive for the first time. Unless you have been a visitor some where recently, you may have forgotten how difficult it is to visit a new group.

People often put off going to a new group for several weeks because of two fears: The fear of the unknown (they simply don't know what to expect); and the fear of rejection (one of the most common fears that keep people from going to a new group). Therefore, single adult leaders must pull out all the stops to make visitors feel wanted and welcome. (I offer specific suggestions on welcoming visitors later in this chapter.)

THE VISITOR

People visit singles groups for a myriad of reasons. When working with single adults, keep in mind that they are a diverse group of people. Most of them fall into one of the following three categories of visitors.

The Shoppers

These are visitors who check out the group to see if it fits their social needs. They are primarily "window shopping" and are often more interested in finding a date for the weekend than becoming a part of the group. They look around and, if they don't discover anybody interesting, they'll usually move on next week and check out a different group.

The Seekers

These visitors are genuinely interested in seeking new friendships and in finding some wholesome activities in which to participate. They are more interested in commitment and developing in-depth relationships.

The Sorrowers

These visitors have recently experienced a major loss in their lives. They have just experienced a divorce or are going through one now, or they are recently widowed. These visitors are the "walking wounded." They may feel hopeless and totally devastated. Some of these people wonder if life is still worth living and have contemplated suicide. These visitors are "critical care patients" in our singles groups—they deserve extra support and attention.

One way to distinguish between the shopper and the seeker is by the type of questions they ask before coming to the meeting. The shopper is more interested in knowing about the people who attend—how many attend and how old are they. The seeker wants to know about the programs and often wants to know what the single adult ministry has to offer his or her children.

Another way of putting it is that some visitors are looking for "action," while others are looking for activities and associations. The shopper always takes from the group whatever fits his or her needs; the seeker eventually gives back to the group personal time and service. The first seldom makes firm commitments to the group; the second is a future leader.

A sorrower is a visitor with a need to tell you about his or her pain. She may call to ask about the program but quickly start talking about her divorce, or he may drop by to chat but really wants to talk about how much he misses his deceased spouse. These people begin to recover from their loss when they no longer have a compulsion to tell everybody about their sorrow.

My own philosophy is that I'm glad single adults visit our group regardless of their reasons. After my own divorce, I thought I needed a fuller social life. I was a taker. When my wounds started healing, I was able to give again.

Understand the different reasons why people visit singles groups, and be glad they came to "check it out." And while they are with you, hope they will come to like the people they meet as well as the programs. Don't be discouraged if many first-time visitors don't come back. The rule of thumb is that about 50 percent of them won't return. On the other hand, about 50 percent do return to become vital members of the single adult ministry.

Welcoming and Incorporating Visitors

What do single people feel is important in a church? Single adults want to feel welcome and affirmed. Visitors must feel welcome and comfortable as soon as possible. This is called "incorporation." It is "the process of helping newcomers feel socially comfortable with the church, its people, programs, and facilities," writes Dr. Bill Sullivan in *Small Group Newsletter*. First-time visitors are "unfamiliar with the context and unacquainted with your members," says Sullivan. He continues, "Such a situation naturally creates social discomfort. If that discomfort remains at the conclusion of the first contact, the likelihood of the newcomer returning drops markedly."[1]

But how does a single adult ministry make people feel welcome? Have an official welcome table at the entrance to the room, where visitors are greeted and offered promotional literature along with a name tag and a handshake. Some groups have a form for the visitor to complete. As visitors fill in the information, the greeter makes their name tags. (A good visitor's form is simple to complete and doesn't ask for much information because it may intimidate the visitor.) People working the welcome table must have an outgoing, pleasant personality and realize that visitors are often very apprehensive about going to a singles function.

Also consider using "secret greeters." Visitors expect to be greeted by an official greeter. No big deal, the visitor thinks, that was their job. Really impress visitors by training a few secret greeters to roam the room looking for visitors to make them welcome with friendly conversation. Of course, it would be nice if all members would greet new people, but many regulars have their own social agenda and often overlook newcomers. Therefore, it's a good idea to plant secret greeters who concentrate on meeting visitors.

Choose secret greeters carefully. Look for people with outgoing and friendly personalities, who use good hygiene, and are willing to put the welfare of the group above their own personal interests. They should be sincere but not overly enthusiastic because that can turn people off too. Train secret greeters to help visitors connect with members in similar jobs, of the same age, or with similar hobbies. This allows greeters to move on to talk with other visitors.

Here are additional suggestions offered by Rev. Roger

McCarthy, the singles minister with Singles Alive, Century Assembly of God in Lodi, California.

At Singles Alive we do several things to make our visitors welcome. We have greeters at the door to welcome visitors and have them fill out a registration form. The greeter introduces them to someone to sit by.

We have a favorite song we sing every week during the worship time of our service. At a certain point, everyone gives hugs (anything longer than 3 seconds becomes a mug). During the announcement time, the visitor is introduced to the entire group by the person they were introduced to at the door.

Visitors are personally invited to go with our singles to our Afterglow (our fellowship and social time). Sometimes we have our Afterglow on the premises and sometimes at our favorite restaurant. If the visitor makes a new friend, we know they'll be back. The following week we send visitors a welcome letter telling them what Singles Alive is all about and inviting them to continue to attend and make new friends. We often have one of our trained leaders or myself call or visit visitors as a further follow-up.

Follow-up with Visitors and Inactives

Church growth experts say it is important for the church to follow up and make contact with visitors within a few days after their visit on a Sunday morning. Here is an example of follow-up procedures for visitors to a single adult Sunday school class. The follow-up chairperson writes down the name and phone number from the visitor's form each visitor completed and calls them within a couple of days. If a special event is coming soon, the chairperson encourages the visitor to attend and explains how to register or reserve a place. Visitors will probably welcome a phone call, but not an unannounced visit. If your group representatives want to visit visitors, call first to make an appointment.

The staff person or singles leader sends a welcome

letter the next day, if possible, and adds a personal note in pen at the bottom of the letter. Enclose a survey with the letter that invites the visitor to indicate his or her interests in various types of activities the singles group regularly offers. The survey also has a place for comments where the visitor may write feedback about attending the class.

Invite all visitors for the month to a hospitality dinner or dessert for first-timers. At the event, explain various programs and encourage visitors to keep coming to the group. Invite the officers to attend and have photo albums of activities available so the visitors can see pictures of past activities. Pass out the newsletter and talk about a few upcoming activities and policies (such as child care, making reservations for activities, or smoking). Include enough time for socializing and refreshments. Implementing such a follow-up procedure increases the chances of visitors becoming active members of the single adult ministry.

It is often more difficult to follow up with absentees. But a good follow-up system does encourage absentees to return—often they just need to be nudged a bit.

The secretary, who keeps the attendance records and notices an absentee pattern, calls it to the attention of the follow-up committee. They assign someone to make a phone call, write up a summary of the conversation, and report the results to the singles minister or follow-up committee.

Don't give up on absentees; show them the singles group still cares by following up and staying in touch.

Research suggests that a new member must be able to identify with approximately seven friends in the church, or the person is likely to become inactive.[2] The article "Can We Close the Back Door" claims that "friendships appear to be the strongest bond cementing new members to their congregations."

This is particularly true within singles groups. Many singles desperately need friendships. If they don't develop friendships soon, they are likely to move on in their search for a singles group that feels warm and inviting. "The first three to six months are crucial," the article says of new converts. Those who have made few or no friends during that time "are on their way out the back door." For singles, the time period can be as short as three to six weeks!

So, to turn visitors into members of the single adult ministry, help them to develop meaningful friendships with other members in the group. Use an active welcoming committee, good follow up, a friendly atmosphere, and activities that encourage maximum interaction with everybody.

THE "ALUMNI"

One of the most important questions all singles groups face is whether to allow single members who marry to remain in the group. Many singles insist that their newly married friends be allowed to remain in the single adult ministry. While the group may dearly love the new couple and want to continue having them in the group, it is not good for anyone concerned. It is not good for the group because gradually allowing singles who marry to remain transforms the group into something other than a pure singles ministry. Soon the group may have a number of married couples in it and, as nice as they are, they become a detriment to attracting new single people to the group.

Neither is it good for the newly married couple. They need to move on to a couples group or class and build friendships with other couples. I occasionally wonder about the motives of married couples who want to remain in a singles group—could there be some insecurity there that keeps them involved?

Ease the Exit

Many singles groups have disintegrated because they allowed their married friends to remain in the group. With this in mind, I offer a few suggestions for gently moving the newlyweds out of the singles ministry while maintaining occasional contact with them once they have "graduated." Some singles groups affectionately term newlyweds "alumni" to describe their members who get married. Provide a graceful transition for alumni. They have happy memories of the group and will be among the ministry's greatest supporters—again, "The best advertising is a satisfied customer."

Give newly married alumni a class gift. If your group has a lot of weddings, find a universal gift suitable for all couples getting married. The gift is given to the couple at their wedding on behalf of the entire singles group.

The last time the couple are in the class before getting married, invite them to come forward at the end of the meeting for people to come by and offer them their best wishes.

Suggest some new classes and groups for alumni to attend. Have an active married couple actually take the new couple around to the various couples classrooms to show them where these groups meet. Even though the newlyweds are no longer eligible for the singles class, they are made to feel wanted by representatives of the married classes.

Remembering Your Former Members

Have an alumni photo album on display in class which contains pictures of the newlyweds as members of the singles group. Their picture in the album assures the couple that they are still cared for and will be remembered by single friends.

Once a year have a reunion dinner or party and invite

all alumni of the single adult ministry to attend. Have the most recently married couple cut a union cake. If you have videos of past events, reminisce by showing a video at the party.

On the first anniversary of their wedding, remember to send alumni an anniversary card and let them know that you are thinking about them and hope that they are doing well.

More that anything else, with "tentative" or former group members, we must assure them of our love. Whether they have been with our group practically forever or have just walked in today, they need to feel loved and wanted.

▲

PART TWO

Practical Programs

CHAPTER **11**

▲

The Single Adult Sunday School Class

I believe most churches in the country can sponsor a single adult Sunday school class, church school class, or Bible class. Two exceptions are churches that are very small and simply don't have enough singles to work with; and those churches in areas of low growth where visitors are rare. However, I advise all other churches to create a special Sunday school class for single persons. Small churches can begin with one class for singles of all ages and categories—divorced, widowed, and never married. Large churches can begin with two or more classes divided by age group. Do not divide classes according to categories. In other words, don't put divorced people into one class, widowed in another, and never-marrieds in a third class. Division by category tends to create walls between groups. You may offer a support group for divorce recovery—but offer it at a different time from Sunday school classes.

Sunday school classes are the salvation—emotionally and spiritually—of many single adults. Singles who come to church like to have a small group of friends to connect with. They want to associate with those who understand their problems and can speak to their needs. And they want the stimulation and spiritual growth a Sunday school class provides. In other words, a good singles Sunday school class, which also offers various outside activities, is just the fellowship group many singles are looking for and need.

However, don't be discouraged if some of the long-term singles in your church do not get excited about the new class for single adults. The reason for their lack of interest, even resistance, is that they are already attached to a Sunday school fellowship or they have been single long enough that they don't feel the need for a Sunday school class for singles only. Still, once they see all the fun things the new class does, they may eventually start coming to some of the activities and to the class itself.

While you might not be able to persuade the "established single" to come to the new group, you are really targeting two groups of singles—the new singles moving into your area and the many singles who are recently divorced or widowed and are hungry for such a loving and caring fellowship.

THE LOCATION

Location is fairly important for the new single adult Sunday school class to be successful. Lobby the powers that be for the best, most comfortable room in the building.

Asking for the best starts the negotiating for space at the top, increasing your chances of getting a good room. Wanting the best sets the tone for the new class and gives it dignity and status. Both are necessary for the class to succeed.

THE CLASS SESSION

Some Sunday school leaders are purists. They believe

the Sunday morning class is a time to study the Bible
and nothing else. These leaders lecture from the moment the class begins until the bell sounds. Even for the
serious Bible student, a Sunday school can offer a lot
more than just a lecture. Here are some suggestions for
making class time stimulating.

Arrange the seats to create a sense of togetherness,
as in a horse shoe arrangement. People generally like
to be seated so they can see each other. If possible,
position the chairs around tables for people to place
their coffee as well as their Bible and other study
materials.

The room itself should be attractive, the seats comfortable, the lighting sufficient, and the temperature
pleasant. Decorate with seasonal or thematic center-
pieces on the tables to add a bit of atmosphere to the
room. Good class sessions employ good room dynamics.
Make the atmosphere of the room appealing and inviting.

Have a secret greeter lingering near the entrance to
greet all people, especially visitors. This person wears a
regular name tag, not one that says "greeter." They
serve secretly or unofficially, without public recognition
of their function.

Position a welcome table near the entrance. Issue
name tags, various handouts, and activity calendars.
The person manning the table helps newcomers fill out
a brief visitor's form and makes them a special visitor's
name tag. Have coffee, orange juice, and/or doughnuts
available early to entice people to arrive early. Invite
regulars to sign up to bring the treats so each week is
covered. Churches usually furnish the coffee, but the
orange juice may be purchased from the class treasury.

Use a microphone if necessary. While people with a
booming voice can be heard by the entire group, soft
voices will not be heard. Have a class bulletin board and

post notices, sign-ups, wedding invitations, thank you notes, and other information relevant to the class.

When using visual aids, position them so all can see. And when writing anything on the blackboard, write high on the board and in large letters so those in the back of the room can see.

Create a smooth flowing outline of the morning agenda. Here is a typical outline that you can use as a guide:

> Opening welcome and prayer
> Introduction of vistors
> Announcements
> Monthly "extras"
> Devotion and prayer circle
> Short break
> Lesson
> Closing prayer and dismissal

Here's a fuller explanation on how to keep the above agenda fresh and make it interesting from month to month.

Start the class session with a warm welcome and a short prayer. Acknowledge visitors in a positive, non-threatening manner. Sing one or two uplifting Christian choruses. Have fun singing seasonal songs at appropriate times (an Irish ballad near St. Patrick's Day, a patriotic song near July 4, etc.).

Give announcements the attention they deserve, but make them snappy. Make announcements verbally and in writing. Write an outline of activities for the week in one corner of the blackboard. Should an activity be scheduled that did not appear on the calendar, print the details of the activity on paper and distribute it at the appropriate time. With lots of other announcements being made, the details of the new activity may get lost in the shuffle.

When making verbal announcements, give "persuasion statements" instead of simply reciting the facts regarding activities. People need to be persuaded by an interesting announcement. Persuasion statements make the activity intriguing and spark interest.

If class time exceeds an hour, take a short break. A short break allows people to stretch their legs, get some coffee, and socialize a bit, before reassembling for the lesson.

Each class session could include a short devotion and prayer time. The devotional leader takes prayer requests and praises, then leads the class in prayer. Vary the traditional Sunday school routine with monthly "extras." Extras occur during the class before the devotion and prayer circle. Here are some suggestions.

First Sunday

Print all birthdays on the monthly calendar and invite people with birthdays to come forward and receive a birthday ribbon while their class mates sing "Happy Birthday" (you can insert "God bless you" in place of individual names).

Second Sunday

Arrange to interview a different class member each month. Ask questions that provide information and background on the person being interviewed. Ask about birthplace, education, career, family, hobbies, and favorite class activities. Interviews help classmates to get better acquainted.

Also consider doing a monthly "Show and Tell." Volunteers bring something they made to the class and talk about it and share an interesting side of themselves.

Third Sunday

Invite a chairperson of a church department to give a brief overview of their department and how it affects the single adult Sunday school class.

Fourth Sunday

The following month's activity calendar is distributed in class on the fourth Sunday of the month. Point out the highlights of the coming month's activities, noting any events that have deadlines needing advance reservations.

Fifth Sunday (Once per Quarter)

Surprise the class with a five-minute cameo appearance by other staff persons in your church or other lay leaders. During their cameo appearance, guests deliver a brief message or song for the class.

Sunday school should be fun. Add spice to the class with brief games such as an occasional attendance contest that awards prizes to winners. Or write a quote on the blackboard leaving out an important word. Invite the class to fill in the blank. For example, "God could not be everywhere, so he created_____." (The answer is "Mothers.") Award the winner with a free coupon to a future event the group plans to attend.

THE LESSON

Those attending a Sunday morning Sunday school usually expect to hear a Bible lesson. There are three basic types of Bible study: topical studies that trace certain subjects such as faith, love, evil, sin, forgiveness, divorce, or remarriage throughout the Bible; character studies of major biblical figures; and book studies that focus on a particular book in the Bible such as the minor prophets, prophetic books, or prison epistles.

However the Bible is taught, pay particular attention to point out those passages that involve singles or speak to singles issues.

Many special topics concerning single adults can be taught or discussed during the class session. Topics may include single parenting; living single in a couples world; finding fulfillment as a single; coping with life as a single adult; dating and relationship issues; and intimacy. Plan occasional discussions on these topics. Tie the discussion to relevant Scripture verses on each topic.

Remember, there are a number of special days throughout the year that are opportunities for Sunday school lessons. Both the church calendar and the national calendar offer many appropriate lessons.

Any time you offer a special lesson, series, or guest speaker, give it publicity. The publicity will not only promote the special occasion to the single adult Sunday school class, it also creates interest within the singles community and increases attendance.

One of the cardinal rules of any good Sunday school class is to vary the type of lessons offered. Use your imagination to make the class session interesting. Singles always appreciate good lessons that are relevant to their needs.

At the end of the class time the leader thanks everyone for coming and invites them to stay for worship. Tell visitors that the single adults have a special place to sit together in church (if you do) and that all visitors are welcome to join them for worship.

Exciting Sunday school classes for single adults are possible. Simply do some brainstorming and use a little imagination. And use as many different people as possible in managing each class period so that the Sunday school class is not perceived as a one-person show. The more people who get involved, the more committed they will be.

▲

CHAPTER 12

Support Groups

The growth of support groups has been phenomenal. Reportedly there are more than 200 different kinds of support groups in the United States. Many of these fall into the category of Twelve Step programs, such as Alcoholics Anonymous. These programs are based on the Twelve Step process, which helps people recover from addictions or other debilitating problems.

There are many other types of support groups throughout the country. Three main support groups for single adults are grief support groups (for widowed persons); divorce support groups (for divorced persons or those going through divorce); and single parent support groups. Many churches and mental health organizations across the country have started such support groups. Your local Christian bookstore has many books dealing with divorce or grief recovery.

SPECIAL INTEREST SUPPORT GROUPS

Here are a few helpful singles support groups addresses and phone numbers.

Widowed Persons

The Widowed Persons Service is an outreach program to help widowed persons of all ages. It operates

under the auspices of the American Association of
Retired Persons. Volunteers—themselves widowed persons—offer emotional support and a listening ear. The
Widowed Person Service also offers referrals to appropriate community agencies.

WPS-AARP
601 "E" Street Northwest
Washington, DC 20049
(202) 434-2277

THEOS (They Help Each Other Spiritually) is a national organization which offers grief recovery for
widowed persons. THEOS has more than 100 chapters
in the United States and Canada.

THEOS
1301 Clark Building
717 Liberty Avenue
Pittsburgh, Pennsylvania 15222
(412) 471-7779

Divorced Persons

While there is no national organization, many local
churches and mental health agencies across the country
offer various types of divorce support groups and
recovery programs. For further information, contact
churches and agencies in your area.

Mothers Without Custody

Mothers Without Custody, Inc., is a national organization lending support to four categories of women:
those who have voluntarily given up custody of their
children, those who have lost custody to their ex-hus-
bands in court, women whose children have been stolen
by their ex-spouses, and those whose children have been
taken by the state and put in foster-parent homes or
alternative care.

Mothers Without Custody, Inc.
Box 27418
Houston, Texas 77227-7418
(713) 840-1622

Parents Without Partners

Parents Without Partners (PWP) is an international organization with more than 100,000 members in the United States. Founded in 1957 in New York City, PWP is a support organization for single parents. Their aim is to reshape the lives of single parents and their children through various types of programs and activities for parents as well as their children. There are 700 chapters in the United States and Canada. To locate a chapter near you, look in the phone book under Parents Without Partners or contact their national office.

Parents Without Partners
8807 Colesville Road
Silver Spring, Maryland 20910
(301) 588-9355
or (800) 637-7974 (for membership information only)

Divorced Dads

There is no national organization for divorced dads but there are several loosely connected support groups for divorced fathers scattered throughout the country. To locate them, check the phone book under Divorced Dads, Fathers Rights or some similar name.

National Self-Help Clearinghouse

There are more than 600 self-help groups and organization throughout the nation, far too many to list here. These groups deal with a wide range of concerns, issues, and addictions. For more information contact:

American Self-Help Clearinghouse
c/o St. Clare Riverside Medical Center
Denville, New Jersey 07834
(201) 625-7101

DIVORCE SUPPORT GROUPS

Let's give a little more attention to the needs of a divorce support group. Actually, a lot of the same principles would apply when establishing a support group for any concerns.

Robert Barber says there are a number of things you should consider before you begin a support group.[1] Before creating such a group, a church must deal with two basic questions: "Why offer a divorce support group with a Christian framework?" and "What population does such a group wish to address?"

In answer to the first question, where better to lay the burdens of anger, guilt, and depression than at the feet of Christ? There, divorced people find the source of hope that allows them to move joyfully ahead. And to the second: You probably won't be able to help all of the divorced people in your area. In highly populated areas, a group may choose to limit participation to those in their first year of divorce or only to those with adolescent children. You should exclude married persons who are considering divorce. A divorce support group cannot and should not replace marriage or family counseling. The intent of a divorce support group is not to kill ailing relationships, but to help those whose marriages have irrevocably ended.

As you publicize a new divorce support group, personal contact with fellow pastors and lay leaders is more effective than mass mailings to area churches. And, as with other singles activities, you should also send community service announcements to local television, radio, and newspapers.

The Two Phases of Divorce Support Group Meetings

Now you may wonder, "How should this support group work? How does it function?" There are a few things you should know.

Phase 1: The weekly meeting during the first two months

During the first two months of meetings, you should meet weekly. These meetings should include twenty minutes of information or teaching and forty to fifty minutes of group discussion each week. The facilitator's task is to introduce a relevant topic and provide a safe place for discussion. Once the group is interacting, the leader's responsibility shifts to reflecting feelings and cementing communication.

The people who come may not know each other and may still have strong feelings about their divorce. They may feel victimized or lonely or very angry or they may need help sorting out what they feel. The leader should try to help them relax and get to know one another so they can talk freely.

Informational topics to explore depend upon each group's make-up. Here are a few specific topics that are usually helpful to discuss:

- Divorce is a process that started long before the lawyers were hired and will last for years after the papers are signed.
- A Christian theology of divorce that deals with sin, guilt, and forgiveness.
- The custody, care, and rearing of children in a divorced family.
- Recognizing immediate personal needs and giving them immediate attention.

Phase 2: Balance support with social needs

After the first two months, support meetings occur every other week. A major social activity is scheduled once a month. It's a good idea to invite children sometimes.

At this stage, the group no longer needs the facilitator's opinions; its members can develop their own opinions. Newly divorced people often see themselves as helpless. As they express their feelings and explore new ideas, they come to realize that, through God's grace, they are no longer helpless and that anger can help them grow. Some group members may idealize others as "having it all together." They need to be gently reminded that everyone has struggles and problems.

Guidelines for Facilitating Support Groups

Most of these guidelines were submitted by Rev. Jerry Porter, a Christian Church (Disciples of Christ) pastor in Kansas City who has conducted many support groups following his own divorce. These principles will work for any type of support group.

Each person in the support group must agree not to talk about what is said in the group outside of group meetings. This provides confidentiality and allows for more openness in the group. Outside the group an individual may repeat something he or she said, but must not quote anyone else.

One of the main purposes for a support group is to provide a forum where people can "tell their story" without being judged. However, the group does have permission to gently alert each other and the facilitator when someone is rambling or elaborating too much. No one is to share more than he or she wants to and certainly each one has the right to say, "I pass" or "I can't talk about that now." The facilitator needs permission to keep individuals from sharing things they would regret later.

New members are only brought in by the facilitator. Anyone who knows of someone who may benefit from the group process should encourage that person to discuss the matter with the facilitator. Since most groups have a policy of "closing" after a couple of sessions, new persons can either be referred to another divorce support group in the area or wait until the next one is created.

When a group member wants to stop coming to the support group, it is highly recommended that the group member talk it over with the rest of the group before quitting. This allows all members to work through "closure" when anyone leaves the group. If for any reason a group member must miss a meeting, announce it to the whole group. That member should notify the facilitator before the group meets.

Use the group time for sharing and receiving feedback as well as working through feelings and behavior. Group members may wish to share their home phone numbers with each other on an individual basis. They are then able to lend each other support during the week.

Encourage group members to talk in the first person ("I") when sharing their experiences and to avoid "you" statements, which communicate blame or superiority. This is especially important when giving feedback to each other.

It is essential to honor each other's emotional space. Feelings of being emotionally invaded hurt a person's self-esteem. Allow each person to open up as he or she is able.

Remember to use comfortable chairs and arrange them in a circle so everyone can see everyone else. Provide refreshments for the first meeting and ask members to sign up to bring them to future meetings. Provide child care if necessary. Start and stop on time.

Allow divorced individuals to feel that they belong to their small support group and to the larger single adult ministry. Let them know they are not alone. Remember that the purpose of support groups is to encourage and help one another, not to lecture or stifle or pity. You will know you have succeeded when these hurting people begin to help others.

▲

CHAPTER 13

Activities

There are a variety of activities and events you can plan for the single adult ministry. This chapter should give you some ideas for the categories of socials, dinners, sports, recreation, vacations, service projects, and holiday events.

SOCIAL ACTIVITIES

People of all ages and marital status love to have fun. Give your singles group plenty to do. Social activities often provide more than just a good time of fellowship; for some it's great therapy, especially if they don't get out much. Here are dozens of activities single adults enjoy. Adapt activities to fit the particular needs of your group.

The Numbers Game

If you have a large group that needs more interaction and mingling, play The Numbers Game.

Count the number of people in the room and cut up that many pieces of paper. Divide that number in half and then write duplicate numbers on the pieces of paper starting with number one. When you are through, you should have two sets of each number. In other words, if you have sixty people in the room, you have sixty pieces of paper—two pieces with a number one on them, two with a number two, and so on up to the number thirty.

Put all those pieces of paper with numbers on them into a hat, box, or other small container. Invite everyone to draw out one piece of paper each. When everyone has drawn a piece of paper, ask them to find the other person holding their duplicate number and spend fifteen minutes talking with each other about themselves.

A variation of this is to have numbers one through thirty-two printed up beforehand. Print one set on blue and the other set on pink paper. If fifteen men are present, cut up the fifteen blue numbers in the hat. Do the same for with the pink numbers, and have the women draw. Then each person pairs off with whoever has the matching number. Again, they talk about themselves for fifteen minutes.

Another variation is to limit conversation to five minutes, then switch discussion partners. On the next round, men look for women who have their number, plus one. In other words, the man who is holding the number four looks for the woman with the number five. In this way, the game is played long enough for each person to have four or five discussion meetings within thirty minutes.

Hug Tag

Play Hug Tag just like any other version of tag with one exception. The only time players are "safe" is when they are hugging someone else.

Friday Night Films

A good movie is usually a winner. When the group plans to go to the movies, publicize the movie title in advance as a courtesy to anyone who may have already seen it. Either before or after the movie, plan to meet at a restaurant for a meal or snack.

If the movie is based on a book, encourage the group to read the book before seeing the movie.

Movie parties are always nice, especially when the weather outside is bad and social or recreational options are limited.

View and Chew

View and Chew is a gathering at someone's home to watch a movie on a VCR. Home VCR parties offer informal socializing during the movie and a wider choice of movies. And everyone brings their favorite munchies or a soft drink as refreshments for the evening. There are several variations on home VCR parties. One variation is sharing a potluck dinner first, then watching the movie. Build a theme around the movie you select, and ask everybody to dress accordingly. For example, rent a western movie and ask those attending to wear something western; a detective movie requires participants to dress like their favorite flat foot such as Joe Friday, Dick Tracy, Colombo, or a favorite female suspect.

Select educational films from a number of film and video resource agencies and libraries. Consider videos that deal with such subjects as friendship, decision making, love, relationships, single living, or single parenthood.

Singles Night at the Cinema

Another movie option is to get a local movie theater to host a Singles Night. One single adult group reported that a theater in San Diego did this and hundreds of singles attended. The movie house allowed singles to have a social time before the movie and even furnished popcorn and soft drinks during the movie. Afterward, everyone was invited to an adjacent restaurant for pie and coffee.

A Black and White Party

Simply announce the date, time, and place for a black and white party and that everybody is to come dressed in a black and white costume or uniform. Instead of making black and white dress mandatory, let those in free who come dressed up, but charge the others a small fee.

Here are a few ideas for black and white costumes: referee, judge, baker, chef, chimney sweep, prisoner, doctor or dentist, waiter, nurse, train conductor, orchestra member. Prizes may be awarded to the most creative, unusual, or authentic.

The serious part of the evening begins with an invitation to the party-goers to list issues in life that are either black or white. Some issues that are sure to stir debate are abortion, mercy killing, interracial marriage, or playing the lottery. The point of this is to demonstrate the differences in our value systems—what may be white (right) to some are grey (uncertain) or even black (wrong) to others.

Lip Syncing

Lip syncing is moving your lips in synchronization with a record or tape. Include a lip sync act as part of another program or have a lip sync contest by inviting interested persons to lip sync their favorite song or other recording. Lip syncing is not new. Creators of television commercials occasionally use the technique to hold viewers attention because it is funny to watch someone imitate a familiar recording artist.

Recordings for lip syncing are endless—current pop songs; all-time favorite recordings; classic radio programs like Amos and Andy; and even news commentators like Paul Harvey.

Prizes may be awarded for best performances.

Jokers Wild Party

The Fine Arts Singles group in the Kansas City area has sponsored several Joker's Wild Parties built around telling jokes and funny stories. Here is a sample schedule for a Joker's Wild Party.

7:30-8:00 Attitude Adjustment Period—getting the audience primed and prepared for the evening.

8:00-8:30 Contest #1— General Story Category.

8:30-9:00 Guest Headliner—invite a local comedian to perform.

9:00-9:15 Refreshment Break

9:15-9:45 Contest #2—Personal Story Category.

9:45-10:15 Contest #3—Religious Story Category.

10:15-10:45 Contest #4—Round-Robin Run-Off.

10:45-11:30 Awarding of prizes and refreshment time.

General guidelines for Joker's Wild Parties include wearing costumes and make-up to enhance story tellers chances of winning. Offer prizes, either cash or gifts, for the best performance in each category. Establish a time limit of three to five minutes for each performance. Stipulate no foul language or obscenities.

The round robin format means that each participant wishing to tell a joke during this time must connect it to the previously told joke or story. This allows the audience to participate spontaneously with their own stories or jokes. The prize goes to the one who most often tells a story connected to previous ones.

Announce categories in advance so people can be giving some thought to participating in the event.

Charge a small admission fee to cover the cost of the guest comedian and prizes.

Midwinter Wienie Roast

Tim Jorgensen of the Grace United Presbyterian Church in Council Bluffs, Iowa, said his most unusual singles group activity was a wienie roast over an open fire in midwinter. He says it was very cold and snowy, but very fun. Use picnic tables and pretend it's summer.

A Slice of Summer Fun

A nice title for this event is A Slice of Summertime, and it's open to the entire church family. As you will see, it is a rather ambitious undertaking for a large church or by a number of singles groups participating together for a really fun evening.

Schedule the event from 7 to 9 P.M. with watermelon available during that time. Offer a number of fun workshops that either run continuously during the evening or in blocks of an hour each. Here are several ideas for fun workshops: flower arranging, face painting, how color affects our personality,what's new in video equipment, a public relations film from a local professional sports team, a fashion show, a fitness clinic, or a movie on outdoor sports like water skiing, camping, or hiking.

Sundaes for All

Free Sundaes for All was the offer one singles group made to attract area single adults to an interdenominational social event. The evening consisted of slides, comedy movies, and free sundaes.

Fun with Potatoes

There are probably dozens of ways to incorporate potatoes into a social activity. Here are a few ideas for consideration. Begin a home fellowship with a potato meal. The host bakes the potatoes and the guests bring toppings to share. After the meal, have a theme party, watch a movie on a VCR, or have a game night.

A variation of the above is the host supplies the potatoes and all the trimmings for a fixed fee, followed by a special program or entertainment.

Use the potato meal as a fundraiser. Charge a set price for admission or take up an offering at some point during the meal or entertainment. This produces funds for a small investment on potatoes, toppings, drinks, and dessert.

Light Night

Light Night is a social evening with no "heavy" program—everything is light-hearted.

Invite people to bring table games. Arrange the chairs in one area of the room in a circle for those who wish to sit and talk. A television or stereo also provides light entertainment. And by all means, have plenty of refreshments or have a potluck if you wish. Either way, make sure a variety of food or munchies is offered to fit various diets.

Light Night is a lot of fun, particularly if you have a large group of single people who mix and mingle with each other. But resist the temptation to organize everybody into groups; the evening needs to be loose and freewheeling.

Singles Variety Show

If your group has never sponsored a variety or talent show you'll be surprised at the "ham" that emerges from the most unsuspecting sources. Some singles with serious talent will be delighted to perform.

What a great opportunity to see a different side of people in the singles group. And remember, "A cheerful heart is good medicine" (Prov. 17:22).

Untalent Show

For an evening of laughs, produce an Untalent Show similar to "The Gong Show" of television fame.

We often hear and see the talented people sing and act, now the rest of the singles can get in on the act, clown it up, and have a great time putting on an un-talent talent show.

Brain-Dominance Party

You've probably heard about the right-brain/left-brain theory. There is scientific evidence that substantiates the brain-dominance theory—certain sections of our brain control certain functions or skills. Some proponents of this even divide the brain up into quadrants, not just halves. They talk of an upper left brain, a lower right brain, etc. Supposedly, only about 3 percent of the population is "whole brain," that is, balanced to the point that no quadrant is dominant.

It is important to know that none of these types of domination is wrong; it is just the way we are made. Some people are high in music or interpersonal skills, while others are high in organizational areas. Some are creative; others are logical. Once you understand your own profile, you can better appreciate the differing gifts and strengths of others.

Combine a unique program with a party and invite an authority on brain dominance to present a program on the subject. Those who would like to know their own brain-dominance profile are invited to complete a questionnaire. The authority analyzes the results and produces a graph or profile for each person participating. (The speaker may charge a fee for the analyzing and charting.)

The graph is printed on a 3" x 3" card stock and used as a name tag the night of the party. The speaker gives an overview of the theory and answers specific questions about the individual profiles. Everybody can learn more about themselves and have fun at the party as they talk with each other about their graphs. It is a great conversational tool and makes for an interesting and educational evening.

Cooking Contest and Tasting Party

Have a cooking contest and invite the singles group to sample the entries. Invite all who wish to enter the contest to make their favorite dish and bring it to a specific location by a certain time, when it will be judged. Offer prizes for each of these categories: appetizers, main dishes, salads, vegetables, and desserts. Keep contestants identities secret until judging is over.

Immediately after the judging, single adults sample all the dishes. Afterward, the group may either play some table games or watch a local chef demonstrate helpful cooking suggestions or the latest in culinary techniques.

SUPPERS (AND OTHER MEALS)

Holiday Picnics

Holidays such as Memorial Day, Independence Day, or Labor Day are great times to have singles picnics and outings. These events provide wholesome activities and help fill a real void for single persons who live too far from their families to spend the holidays with them. Smaller singles groups may unite with other singles groups for a larger holiday fellowship.

The Lunch Bunch

One of the most practical activities a church-based singles group can offer its single adults on a regular basis is a Lunch Bunch—a group that eats together after church on Sundays.

Many singles groups across the country have such an activity for their singles. Whether it's called the Lunch Bunch, the Chow Crowd, or a LEO (Let's Eat Out), it's a wonderful activity that doesn't take much energy to plan. During the week, such a meal may be called a

Midweek LEO or a Friday Night LEO or a Saturday Night Special (on a weekend night).

For single adults without families in the area, this time of eating out with friends becomes a treasured alternative to dining alone.

When you promote this event, state whether children are invited. Most dinners out may include children, but occasionally special dinners are for adults only.

Two keys for successful eating-out groups are eating at good restaurants and varying the restaurants. Do not always go to the same place. Nice places with good food attract people and keep them coming back. After all, they are "buying a pig in a poke" when they agree to go to an unknown place for dinner. Respect that and don't let them down.

Mystery Dinners

Have fun with a Mystery LEO where no one but the organizer knows the destination. All you tell the people is how to dress and how much money to bring.

Breakfast/Luncheon Clubs

Create a Singles Breakfast Club. Gather at least monthly to eat breakfast together and hear a speaker. The location is an area restaurant with a meeting room. Advance reservations are required so the restaurant knows how much food to prepare. The speaker should be either someone the group wants to hear or someone presenting a topic of interest to singles. Saturday mornings are an ideal time for breakfast club meetings.

The Luncheon Club is like the Breakfast Club except it meets on a lunch hour during the week. Luncheon Clubs are a little harder to organize because group members work places may be spread over a large area and people have a limited time for lunch.

Dinners for Eight

One excellent way to create fellowship and a better understanding of each other is to eat together. Dinner for Eight (also called a Four by Four Fellowship at one church) allows for four men and four women to share the evening together at someone's home. These dinners are planned monthly; a large singles group may run several dinners simultaneously. Here are a few tips for those who have never organized a Dinner for Eight.

Make a list of everyone interested in participating, keeping the men and women on separate lists. The host or hostess calls the first men and women on each list until four men and four women (including the host or hostess) accept the invitation to dinner. The next Dinner for Eight host or hostess begins calling those who could not attend the previous dinner.

The host or hostess provides the home, menu, and drinks. The host or hostess tells the guests the full menu and what dish to bring. It helps to keep in mind the cooking skills or budget limitations of the guests!

The host or hostess should not serve two months in a row. This gives others a chance to host the dinner and gives themselves an opportunity to be a guest. Guests are encouraged to attend only three times as a guest, and then to host a dinner themselves. Guests may not attend two months in a row unless everyone has had a chance to attend a dinner.

If the host or hostess prefers to buy and serve the meat dish, that person may charge a small fee for the expense. Otherwise, the meat dishes can be assigned to two or three persons, thus dividing the expense evenly.

The host or hostess may offer after-dinner activities at home or suggest they all attend an event of mutual choice.

Dinner for Eight could be expanded to Dinner for Ten or Twelve or restricted to only six people. However, every effort should be made to have a balance of genders.

Guess Who's Coming to Dinner?

Here's another take-off on the Dinner for Eight fellowships. The twist is that no one knows who is coming to dinner—except the coordinator.

A coordinator is selected who lines up hosts or hostesses who determine the menu. That menu is then turned over to the coordinator who assigns dishes to persons invited to attend. The coordinator doesn't reveal who else is coming, thus creating a little suspense.

One coordinator may function for several dinners taking place on the same evening. Naturally, the coordinator should try to strike a balance of men and women so that one group doesn't have all men while the other has all women.

After dinner the guests may join with the other dinner groups meeting that night and participate in another activity together, such as seeing a movie or playing miniature golf. Or if one of the homes is large enough, all may gather at that place for a larger post-dinner games night.

Mystery Guest

Here's another variation on the Dinner for Eight idea. Set an extra place setting for a mystery guest. This mystery person may be someone from the church staff, like the church music director who brings a guitar for an after-dinner sing-along. Or the mystery guest may be someone who has recently taken an exciting trip and brings their slides or videos to show. Perhaps a local celebrity may come to dinner as a favor. Or a person from the singles group is the mystery guest dressed in the costume of a famous person. Or a well-loved alumnus may show up as a surprise. Use your imagination, but keep the mystery guest a secret until the person comes to dinner.

SPORTS AND RECREATION

Singles Night at the Ball Game

If you live in an area with lots of singles groups and a professional sports team, arrange a Singles Night at the ball game. First get the cooperation of other singles groups in your area, then go to the promotions director and bargain for a package of benefits which includes admission to the game and a free soft drink when you buy a hot dog. Even if the promotions director says he or she can't bargain, most will make some concessions if there is the possibility of a large group attending.

The first year we did this in Kansas City, we attended a local professional soccer match. More than 400 single adults attended, representing fourteen different singles groups!

Tennis Parties

Tennis parties are a lot of fun and a great way to meet other single adults who like to play tennis. Reserve a couple of tennis courts for three to four hours. Then invite an equal number of men and women who play tennis. Before they arrive, the party organizer divides players into two blocks—block A plays one session (45 minutes) then sits out while block B plays the next session. They rotate like this all evening.

All matches are mixed doubles. Each person is assigned a new partner for each new session. Players face different opponents each session. If players represent two different skill levels, assign the better players to block A and the others to block B. This makes it more enjoyable for everyone because they play with others of similar skill.

Build a potluck into the evening or perhaps just snacks. The players eat while sitting out. If a lot of singles want to learn to play tennis, talk with a tennis pro who may, for a fee, give lessons to the group.

Sports Challenge

If your group has a number of people who like to play tennis, schedule a match or two with singles from another group. This is a great way for your members to meet other single adults with similar interests. Non players from both groups can shag balls, supply the water, take pictures, or cheer.

Challenge other singles groups to play golf, volleyball, wallyball, softball, or other team sports. (Wallyball is similar to volleyball only played with a softer ball and on an indoor racquetball court. The main difference between the two is that with wallyball you can hit the ball off the walls, thus "wallyball." Check with your local racquetball club for court rental fees and other details.)

Eventually there may be enough interest among singles groups in your area to begin area-wide tournaments in these various sports.

Sports Night: Something for Everyone

In reading a number of singles activity calendars, I noticed that several singles groups have Sports Nights. The singles group goes to a large multi sport facility for an evening of fun and various sports activities. Because the center offers a variety of sports options, the evening attracts more people than one sports event.

For example, some bowling centers also have billiards and/or ice skating available. And some athletic clubs offer swimming, volleyball, wallyball, or ping pong. If

your group is large enough, rent the entire facility just
for your group. Smaller groups may reserve some space
in each sport at the sports center. Afterward, go out for
refreshments unless refreshments are available at the
center.

Battle of the Sexes

With the advent of spring and nice outdoor weather,
a Battle of the Sexes is a good program to hold outside.
Begin with a potluck picnic. After the picnic the sexes
engage in fierce competition in such games as the fris-
bee toss, tug-of-war, chin-to-chin orange or apple pas-
ses, and a water-balloon toss.

Schedule such additional thrilling games as the pan-
cake race, the three-legged race, and the trust walk. The
trust walk consists of a couple who take turns leading
each other blindfolded. Since the couple cannot hold
hands as they walk, the blindfolded person must totally
trust his partner to keep him from walking into trees or
holes. This is a unique experience that brings about
deeper appreciation for our gift of sight.

The Battle of the Sexes picnic concludes with appropriate gag prizes for the winners of various games.
Advance promotion makes this a very popular outdoor
activity.

Backyard Tournaments

Here is a great idea for a summertime fellowship:
Have a backyard volleyball and/or croquet tournament.
Find a person from the group with a large flat back yard
to sponsor a Backyard Tournament. The more agile ones
play volleyball in one area of the yard while the others
play croquet in another area. Be sure to arrange volleyball teams of equal strength.

If there is a large turnout for croquet, have several
heats and a playoff among various heat winners. This

backyard event may be coupled with a barbecue or potluck. Reward the tournament winners by letting them eat first. End the evening by making old-fashioned ice cream served with cake.

Bowling Party

Approach a local bowling lane with a proposal, sponsoring a free bowling party for the single adults in the community. The bowling management agrees to donate up to three hours of free bowling (including shoes) to all singles on a particular night. The benefit to the bowling establishment is that they are allowed to give a pitch that night to single adults interested in joining a bowling league.

SIGHTSEEING

Single adults like to travel but usually not alone. Plan sight seeing trips. These are one-day or weekend trips to historic places or events (ballgames, concerts, theme parks, etc.). Announce the date, time, cost, and transportation well in advance.

Short Trips

For one-day or weekend trips, the trip organizer gathers the necessary information about the trip and fixes a price that covers all expenses. Since people have different eating habits, do not build meals into the price of the trip. This lets people order their own meals to their own satisfaction. The organizer also negotiates group rates for various admissions and lodging if necessary.

Give careful thought to the length of time and the best route for the trip. Make a schedule, and plan to get there in time for the play or concert. Because the organizer must make certain commitments in advance, set a deadline for payment or deposits. Most hotels require a deposit of about 50 percent, due thirty days in advance.

Both day trips and weekenders are a lot of fun. The day trips are easy to organize but weekend trips require a lot more detailed planning.

Group Vacation

When planning a vacation for the entire single adult ministry, work through a travel agent, who offers invaluable assistance to groups planning extended trips.

Multigroup Trip

Several smaller groups may go together on trips. Having other singles groups involved shares organizing assignments. And everyone enjoys making new friends.

One-Day Mystery Trip

Plan a mystery trip. No one but the planner knows where the group is going. Publicity and promotion for the event provides a little information, but never gives away the destination. However, the group needs to know how much money will be needed and how many meals will be offered. Also tell them how to dress—casual, sporty, dressy, etc. Naturally, the destination should be a place that not only surprises them, but also makes them glad they signed up for the trip. Mystery trips should be one-day events, leaving in the morning and returning in the afternoon or evening.

Cruise Party

Plan a Bon Voyage Party. Invite a local travel or cruise agent to talk about all the aspects of cruising—dress codes, tipping customs, ship talk, and shipboard activities.

Some cruise agents arrange singles cruises and love

to give away door prizes to encourage more single adults to come to the program. They are eager to promote their singles cruises and are happy to provide a program for the evening.

One such party was held in the cruise office itself. The office was decorated as a mock-up of a cabin. The cruise agent showed a cruise video which was educational and entertaining.

SEASONAL ACTIVITIES

There are a number of activities that are unique to certain seasons of the year. Here are a few ideas for seasonal activities.

Souper Bowl Sunday

With all the hype given to the Super Bowl every January, plan a party to watch the game and call it Souper Bowl Sunday. Admission is one can of chunky-style soup. The cans are donated to an agency in your community that helps feed the hungry.

Here are a few slogans that the Village Presbyterian Church in Prairie Village, Kansas, used one year to promote a similar event: "Let's Tackle Hunger," or "Let's 'Sack' the Soup and Shut Out Hunger."

To give attendees something to snack on during the game, ask that they bring some munchies or soft drinks to share during the game.

T.G.I.F. Party

As April 15 draws near, more and more people give their attention to filing tax returns. One program idea that has been successful with various singles groups in the past is having a program built around tax information.

Invite a local tax expert to present a program that deals with some of the specific tax concerns of singles, especially single parents. Many people actually prepare their taxes in January and February, so plan the program for early February.

A month later have a T.G.I.F. party. T.G.I.F. stands for "Thank God It's Filed." Those who have filed their returns get in free, those who haven't filed by the time of the party pay a small fee to cover the expense of the party.

Ask creative people in the group to design catchy graphics and decorations for the party using a tax theme.

Here are a few more ideas that have seasonal possibilities. A few have already been described in this chapter. Use blank lines to add a few of your own ideas.

Winter Activities (primarily December through February)

Christmas pageant
Christmas caroling
Gift Exchange
Hockey Games
Basketball games
Snow skiing
Valentine banquet or Party

Holiday brunches or potlucks
Ice skating
A performance of Handel's
    Messiah
New Years Day bowl games
New Years Eve Party

Spring Activities (primarily March through May)

Easter Eve fellowship
Golf
Picnics
St. Patrick's Day party

T.G.I.F (taxes) party

Summer Activities (primarily June through August)

Baseball games
Beach Party
Camping
Cookout/barbecue
Croquet party
Theme parks
Water sports (skiing, swimming, canoeing)
Yard parties

Fireworks viewing
Ice cream social
Joy songs or caroling
Outdoor plays, musicals, or concerts
Riverboat ride

_____
_____
_____
_____

Fall Activities (primarily September through November)

Fall football
Football games
Halloween party
Hayride

Octoberfest
World Series viewing

_____
_____

This is a partial list of seasonal activities. Needless to say, there are a host of outdoor activities. And there are even more indoor activities such as VCR parties, table games, and dinners. Add your favorite seasonal activities and those activities that are unique to your area and community on the blank lines at the end of the lists. Following is a list of even more activities you can do as a group. Add your own ideas at the end.

Airplane show
Art museum
Auction
Bicycle rides
Bowling party
Car show
Car rally
Chili party
Circus
City market
Comedy club
Cookie Bake
Cooking class
Cruise party
Dances (sock hop,square dance etc.)
Dinner theaters
Dinner for eight
English Tea party
Ethnic festival
Fairs (state/county)
Fireside chat
Flower/garden show
Gospel concert
Historic church tour
Historic trips/tours
Horse and dog races
House parties

Ice Capades
Jazz festival
Melodrama
Movies
Mystery trip
Pizza party
Rap/disscussion night
Retreats/advances
Rodeos
Scenic tours
Symphony concert
Talent/untalent show
Train show
Train ride (Amtrak)
Trivial Pursuit party
Trolley ride
VCR party
Wallyball
Western party
Zoo

_____
_____
_____
_____
_____
_____
_____
_____

SPECIAL SINGLE ADULT DAYS

Singles Day

Many churches and even a few denominations now recognize single adults by proclaiming certain days to be Singles Day or Singles Week. The Assemblies of God sponsored their first national Singles Day on November 4, 1984. Their objective got plenty of denominational promotion in their in-house publications. The denominational publications even created clip art for local churches to use. The purpose of Singles Day was "to focus on singles who are making a positive contribution to their churches," said David Reddout, former single adults consultant with the denomination. Singles Day has now become an annual event with the Assemblies of God.

The Southern Baptists often designate one Sunday a year to be Single Adult Day. Their purpose is "to give recognition to all single adults to increase church awareness of single life and to strengthen the church community population." In some of these churches, single adults participate in a number of worship responsibilities on that day. Further activities include a church wide luncheon for singles and a special fellowship after the evening service.

Countless other churches across the country have designated one Sunday each year to honor their single adults. My own church sponsors a Single Sunday held near the anniversary of our first single adult Sunday school class.

Here are a few suggestions for sponsoring a Singles Sunday in your church. Pick a date that does not conflict with any other major promotion within the life of the congregation. Choose a month without any other special days—if possible, stay away from February, May, June, November, and December.

Book a guest speaker for the single adult class.

Schedule a time in the worship service for a brief talk by one of the singles leaders. Ask group members to sit together in the worship service and stand to be recognized when called upon by the leader or the pastor who affirms the singles ministry from the pulpit.

Plan a large single adult lunch after church. The lunch may take place in the church fellowship hall or at a nearby restaurant that can accommodate the crowd.

During the week plan a giant anniversary dinner, complete with group games and a birthday cake, singing

"Happy Birthday to Us" as you eat. This is a great time to share group photos and show videotapes of past activities. Promote the anniversary event to all your singles and alumni. Invite your former singles (now married) to participate in the celebration, and invite them to bring and show off their children.

Not only have churches begun to recognize single adults, but cities and states have also. The mayor of Columbus, Ohio, has often proclaimed a Columbus Singles Day for that town. This was done at the urging of the Buckeye Singles Council, a cluster of singles groups in and around that city, which was also instrumental in getting a National Singles Week proclaimed in Ohio and Utah.

Single Parents Day

Parents Without Partners, an international organization of single parents, was instrumental in introducing a resolution into Congress in the early 1980s calling for a Single Parents Day:

> Whereas there are 14,000,000 single parents in the United States, the number doubling in the past 10 years; Whereas 20 percent of all our Nation's children will live with a single parent before the age of 18.

> Whereas single parents have struggled courageously to raise their children to a healthy maturity, with the full sense of being loved and accepted as persons, and with the same prospects for adulthood as children who mature with their two parents together; and Whereas it is time to recognize the courage and dedication of these parents who work to maintain strong family units to be responsible members of American society; Now, therefore, be it Resolved, that it is the sense of the House of Representatives that March 21, 1984, should be designated "National Single Parent Day." The President is requested to issue a proclamation calling upon the people of the

United States to observe that day with appropriate
ceremonies and activities.

Ex-Spouse Day

A Kansas City minister, Rev. Roger Coleman,
proclaimed Good Friday of each year to be Ex-Spouse
Day to promote the concept of "faithfully divorced."

Rev. Coleman, himself a divorced and remarried person, said, "To be faithfully divorced is to recognize that,
while the marriage has ended, responsibilities to each
other and to the children continue. It also implies that
former spouses, whose actions may have made the marriage unbearable, remain . . .persons worthy of care and
concern. Such acknowledgement of value comes the
closest to what it means to forgive one's ex-spouse."

Good Friday was chosen because of its emphasis on
suffering, isolation,and hopelessness—all feelings involved in a divorce. Following Good Friday, however, is
the faith of Easter which proclaims that separation is
not the final condition and that hope, new life, and love
prevail.

Here are two things Rev. Coleman hopes to ac-
complish on this day which have gained nationwide
attention:

- Encourage responses to former husbands and
  wives that bridge hostility and open up communication, thereby freeing each from emotional
  bondage to the other.
- Increase awareness of the importance of support
  for persons experiencing divorce and promote
  knowledge of available resources, particularly
  small groups in which participants share common
  concerns.

And here are a few of the ten ways Rev. Coleman
suggests to celebrate Ex-Spouse Day.

- Take an ex-spouse to lunch.

- Return to your ex-spouse jewelry, record albums, pictures, or furniture kept out of spite rather than need.
- Add a bonus to your child-support payment.

(For a complete set of materials on Ex-Spouse's Day send a SASE to Rev. Roger Coleman, 706 West 42nd St., Kansas City, MO 64111.)

HOLIDAYS

The Christmas Season

The Christmas holidays are often a depressing time for single persons. For many singles the Advent season of joy and cheer is nothing but a time of dark and drear. It is often a reminder of the ghosts of holiday's past, with all the traditions and memories of when the family was happy together. It is an especially devastating time for single parents going through Christmas for the first time without their children around them to enjoy the festivities.

Many single adults don't have close ties, either with relatives or friends, to help sustain them through Christmas. A lack of a social or familial network leaves many unmarried people feeling depressed during the Christmas season. With little or no support system, many just can't face the holidays alone. It is no wonder then that this season of the year sees more suicides than at any other time of the year. To help single adults not only survive but actually look forward to these days, here are a few suggestions.

- Help your single adults develop a game plan for combating the holiday blahs. By penciling in various activities on their calendar, they can look forward to attending those events. Half the battle is having a schedule of activities that include friends.

- Offer group discussions centered around the theme Handling the Holidays. Offer sensible suggestions that help single adults cope with their feelings and get into the spirit of the celebration.
- Plan activities on the actual holiday. For example, on the morning of Thanksgiving, Christmas, and New Year's, plan to have brunch together around 10 A.M. at a nice restaurant. Also, plan a potluck dinner in the mid afternoon, followed by table games or watching football on television. These brunches give persons living alone a reason to celebrate the holiday.
- Offer group Christmas shopping early in the season so singles can enjoy the parties when they roll around.
- Have a group tree-decorating party for a member or friend that is disabled. Or sponsor a progressive dinner and decorate at each member's house you go to.
- Go caroling at a nursing home, children's home, retirement center, or hospital.
- For single parents, have the church provide child care while the single parents go out shopping.
- Bake cookies and take them to shut-ins or other needy persons in the community.
- Write and send group letters to those members who can't be home for Christmas or who have moved away. Or send a group letter to the church staff and missionaries.
- Encourage volunteers to host an activity. This is the season for giving, not just going to other people's parties. The process of hosting an activity helps single adults get into the spirit of the season.

In the midst of all holiday activities, celebrate life in

Christ and appreciate your relationships with each other as brothers and sisters in the same family.

When Christmas and New Year's days fall on Sunday, don't cancel class or the after-church lunch for singles. Many will be hungry for the fellowship as well as the food.

And finally, here are three things that Dennis Apple, former director of the single adult ministry for the Church of the Nazarene International, says that singles can focus on during the Advent season:

1. Serve and surprise people. Do it anonymously.

2. Watch your schedules. The holiday season is a time of extremes. Some people have too much time on their hands, others too little.

3. Concentrate on making the spirit of giving a way of life throughout the entire year.

New Years Eve

One of the toughest evenings of the whole year for single adults, particularly divorced people, is New Year's Eve. This occasion often brings back memories of previous celebrations when the family was together and times were happier.

Singles groups throughout the country can provide a real and a practical ministry by planning a fun and wholesome activity on New Year's Eve. Begin with a potluck dinner followed by fun and games. If the individuals in your group made New Year's resolutions a year ago and saved them, this is a great time to open them and see who kept their resolutions. Then, just before midnight, turn on the TV and watch the festivities at Times Square in New York City as the people there count down and celebrate the coming new year.

Or you can get together with other singles groups and rent a meeting room at a nice restaurant or a large suite at a beautiful hotel and throw a more elegant party. Or perhaps a single in your group is a member of the local country club and can help you reserve a room there for a New Year's Eve celebration. Party-goers buy tickets to attend. Or there may be a fire works display somewhere in your area; find a good spot where your group can enjoy the show.

Whatever you do, do something creative that will bring single adults and their families together at this special time. Help turn a potentially dreaded time into one of fun and joy!

Valentine's Day

Many churches plan Valentine Banquets for their congregations. Here are some guidelines for attracting single adults to such an event.

Don't call the event a Sweetheart Banquet. Many single individuals do not have sweethearts to bring to the banquet. A Valentine Banquet is not as intimidating.

Price your tickets individually, with no premium for couples and no penalty for singles. In other words, if the tickets are $10 each, they should be $20 for couples, not $18. If the tickets are priced $20 per couple, individual tickets should be $10 for singles, not $11.

Announce in advance that there will be a special singles table at the banquet. Some single adults feel more comfortable sitting with other singles rather than with married couples.

Halloween

Some groups wonder what to do with Halloween. According to some sources, Halloween was originally a holy day, though it certainly bears no semblance to one now. In addition to the standard costume party, here are several suggestions from other groups celebrating Halloween.

A group in Wichita celebrates the day with a Hallelujah Party. Those who attend come dressed as a Bible character instead of in typical Halloween costumes. A prize is awarded for the most authentic-looking costume.

Another group sponsored Halloween in the Graveyard and visited the graves of prominent citizens from their city. They recalled some of the citizens more notable accomplishments at each grave. (Advance permission maybe required from the cemetery management.)

Another group had a Witch Hunt, a variation of the standard scavenger hunt. Those attending this event were divided into teams, each with a camera, and were sent out to take pictures of anything with the word witch in it or anything that rhymes with it (like sandwich or pitch). It was a fun evening that involved a lot of creativity in finding things that rhymed with the word witch. The members of the winning team received prizes.

SPECIAL EVENTS

Singles Information Fair

If your area has lots of singles organizations, have your singles group host an area-wide Singles Information Fair. Though called by different names,several of these exist throughout the country. They all invite business organizations, singles groups, and individuals with unique hobbies to rent booths to display their products and brochures.

Some fairs have special speakers or entertainment which brings in a larger crowd. Clowns are always an added attraction along with door prizes and drawings for valuable items. A free literature table contains various singles publications and other information pertinent to single adults. (If you wish to buy a Singles Information How-To packet which gives many helpful hints, guidelines, sample letters, and advertising brochures, send $5 to: Institute of Singles Dynamics, P.O. Box 11394, Kansas City, MO 64112. Ask for the Fair Packet.)

Drama Resource

Does your singles ministry have a drama group? If not, you might be surprised at how many thespians are in your group. Good drama presentations with a message are a great extracurricular activity for single adults. There are dramas that are general plays and others that deal with seasonal themes. Some use puppets and others focus on special days and occasions. There are dramatic musicals as well as comedy sketches. (The Lillenas Publishing Company offers a catalog of plays. Write to them at P.O. Box 527, Kansas City, MO 64141.)

Seminars and Conferences

Many singles groups across the country sponsor seminars and conferences. Some of these are one-day events, others cover several days, and a few are scheduled over a long holiday weekend so that singles have more time together.

Invite a well-known speaker to deliver the keynote speech on a subject of interest to single adults. Then plan lots of different workshops for the singles to attend according to their interests. Workshop topics range from finances to single parenting, from enjoying single life to divorce recovery, from single parenting to how to deal with loneliness. Most of these events share a main theme and corresponding artwork for publicity.

Unless the sponsoring group is a very large one, organizers usually rely on area singles to attend and offset the financial cost of the keynote speaker, workshop leaders, and promotional expenses. If you intend to invite other groups to this event, give them a couple of months advance notice so they can clear their calendars for it.

Retreats

Most groups offer retreats for their single adults—a time to go away for a day or so to relax and reflect. Also called "advances," this is an excellent time to recharge spiritually. Church groups generally pick a theme dealing with spiritual growth.

One of the main ingredients of a retreat is a special guest or featured speaker. Often this person is an expert with drawing power to attract more singles to the retreat. If you have a small budget, invite a local person to be the keynoter. If you have a big budget, you may be able to afford to fly in a well-known speaker.

Another key ingredient to the retreat is time for sharing and discussion. If the speaker's presentation doesn't include discussion, schedule discussion time after sessions that deal with the speakers topic or other subjects of interest to singles.

Music is also an important ingredient for a successful retreat. Have someone bring a guitar and sing camp songs, hymns, and spirituals.

And remember that one of the hidden agendas for single adults is socializing to get to know other singles and build relationships. Plan time for this. Allow free time and time for recreation.

Location is very important. Don't plan a retreat so far away that you spend most of the time traveling. And stay away from the church building or someone's house. Church campgrounds are a popular place to hold a retreat because the serene setting of most camps lends itself to the purpose of the retreat—to get away from the sights and sounds of the city.

Lodging is another item to consider. The advantage

to most camps is that they offer inexpensive dormitory accommodations. However, if you wish comfort and convenience, hold the retreat in a hotel or at a resort with several persons sharing a room. Remember, the more expensive the lodging, the higher the cost of the retreat. Some of your single adults may not be able to afford an expensive retreat very often. But once in a while, go first class and plan a luxury retreat.

Plan a variety of retreats throughout the year. Plan a one-day retreat (with no overnight) in the spring, then an overnight in the autumn—a beautiful time for a retreat. Plan an annual retreat with just the singles group. Later plan a multi church retreat, and invite other singles groups to join you.

Musical Concerts

One of the most effective ways to get single adults in the community to come back to church is to sponsor a concert or a seminar, according to a book entitled Single Adults in America.[1] Since many single adults are turned off by church, one way to get them interested again is to use a back-door approach. "Back-door" evangelism gets people involved in something else, either held at the church or sponsored by the church. Many people come back to church as a result of this kind of evangelism. In fact, when researchers with the Barna Group asked single adults what would get them interested in church, singles said the best way was to send them a cassette tape of a typical service or to have the church sponsor a musical concert or a seminar open to the public.

While concerts and seminars have intrinsic value in themselves, their long-range value is that some of those who attend might eventually return for a worship service. I believe that churches offering such programs are usually the churches experiencing the greatest growth in membership.

Consider offering a concert at the church on a regular basis as outreach to single adults in your community.

These ideas are just a starting place. They should get your juices flowing to invent your own special activities. Get together with your executive board and even the whole singles group, and brainstorm about what you'd like to do together. You may be surprised at the fun you come up with!

CHAPTER **14**

▲

Service Projects

I once heard the Rev. Jim Smoke, nationally known author and singles leader, say that there are two kinds of singles groups: those who give and those who take. The first type encourages its single adults to give and serve each other and others. The second type simply allows its single adults to attend the meetings and soak up the benefits, but doesn't encourage them to give anything back; the meetings are an end in themselves.

A healthy single adult ministry provides a service for those who attend and encourages its members to help others personally as well as through group service projects. With this in mind, the singles group is not only an important meeting for inspiration and fellowship but also a "pit stop" where single adults get filled up to go back out and serve.

GROUP PROJECTS

The following is a list of the various types of service projects available for group participation.

Special Olympics

The Special Olympics for disabled persons is held every year. Many volunteers are needed to keep time, keep score, and help with a multitude of other duties.

For more information, contact the Special Olympics organization in your area.

Singles Exchange

The singles group connected with the Hennepin United Methodist Church in Minneapolis, Minnesota, organized a Singles Exchange Program. The exchange is a system whereby singles exchange services with each other, such as painting, hard work, moving, or child care. Persons interested in getting involved complete a one-page registration form which asks what services they need and what services they have to offer. All information is fed into a computer that furnishes a printout matching services with needs. Once a person has received his or her printout, it is then up to the individual to make contacts and negotiate an exchange that is mutually beneficial.

This is a good system to enable single adults to help each other, save money on needed services, and build a caring network of friends.

Ronald McDonald House

Is there a Ronald McDonald House in your area? If so, contact them and volunteer the single adult ministry to prepare a meal for residents. Each house has a resident house manager plus a team of volunteers who assist in many ways. Their slogan is "Hope Away from Home." Out-of-town families stay here for a nominal fee while their children are hospitalized. However, since there is no food service at the houses, they usually eat at nearby restaurants, which is very expensive. It is a nice gesture for a singles group to prepare enough food for all the families at the house that week.

Dance Donations

Dance Donations is a combination service project and

a fundraiser. The Village Singles of Prairie Village, Kansas, invites singles attending their monthly dances to also bring an item to be donated to their charity of the month. During one year this group collected thousands of items and thousands of dollars for twenty-one community and charitable projects. These items went to such causes as a battered women's shelter, Catholic Social Services, a children's center, the City Union Mission, a couple of churches, and other organizations serving economically deprived persons. Volunteers also donated their time to such causes as Habitat for Humanity, Crop Walk, Lou Gehrig's Disease Association, a weatherization project, Easter Seals, the Salvation Army, and other fundraisers for charity.

Joy Songs

You've heard of Christmas in July—now there are Joy Songs in July. The Unity Singles group in Kansas City goes to local hospitals and nursing homes and sings "joy" songs.

It's great to go Christmas caroling in December, but most hospitals are inundated with groups at that time of the year. For a fresh approach, organize a group to go sing some uplifting, joyful songs during June or July. Everyone will love it.

Round-Robin Letter

"Round-robin" or group letters are a good wintertime service project. First, identify people the group would like to write to—former single adults in your group who have moved far away; missionaries your church supports; or special speakers who have addressed the group. Consider writing those in the hospital or those who have recently lost a loved one. Or surprise your pastor, Sunday school teacher, singles minister, or some other staff person with a group letter on his or her birthday.

After deciding to whom to write, decide whether the letter is to be written on the same card or stationery or whether everyone will write their own letter. Invite participants in the round robin to write their thoughts on the card, stationery, or whatever you decide to use. If everybody writes on the same document, limit it to one paragraph per writer. If everybody wants to write an individual letter, mail the individual letters in one large envelope.

What a pleasant surprise that awaits the chosen recipient!

Summer Service Project

Any single adults fortunate enough to have long summer vacations, but don't know what to do with them, may be interested in spending their time helping others. There is literally a world of opportunities open for those who can afford to donate one or more weeks to some worthwhile cause.

A few opportunities include youth camp, vacation Bible school, team evangelism, teaching and tutoring, and even construction work. For example, Habitat for Humanity is looking for persons to help construct houses for the poor. (Habitat and Church St., Americus, GA 31709; phone: 912-924-6935.)

There are also a number of Christian organizations happy to discuss a compatible summer placement with interested parties. A few of these include:

- InterVarsity Missions, P.O. Box 7895, Madison, Wisconsin 53707
- Intercristo, 19303 Freemont Avenue North, Seattle, Washington 98133 (1-800-426-1342)
- Mobilized to Serve, 7245 College Street, Lima, New York 14485 (716-582-2790)

- Bridge Builders, c/o Chris Easton, 9925 7th Way North #102, St. Petersburg, Florida 33702 (813-576-4152).
- Short-Term Missions Advocates, 919 West Huntington Drive, Monrovia, California 91016

The Short-Term Missions Advocates organization also has a publication entitled Stepping Out: A Guide to Short-Term Missions, which lists more than seventy agencies with hundreds of short-term opportunities available for volunteers who have one or more weeks to donate.

Also, contact the appropriate office at your own denominational headquarters for available work projects.

INDIVIDUAL PROJECTS

In addition to the things single adults can do as a group, individuals may volunteer their services. They can offer their help in remedial reading programs, hospitals, homes for youth, children, and abused women, and a myriad of other organizations.

Individuals also offer to help other individuals. The following is a beautiful example.

On a particular night during the holiday season, a certain lady in the First United Methodist Church of Conroe, Texas, invites the children of single parents to go out shopping with her to buy Christmas presents for their parents. Fortunately, this lady in Conroe has the financial means to buy these presents herself after the children pick them out. What a self-giving, sensitive thing to do for the single-parent families in that congregation!

If your church isn't fortunate enough to have such a person in your membership, modify this idea a bit by asking single parents to provide the money for their presents. Or the singles group may subsidize the gifts for single parents unable to participate otherwise.

Service projects aren't hard to find. There are plenty of needs in your own community. Just look around and use your imagination.

CHAPTER **15**

▲

Fundraising

In a 1990 survey of singles leaders, the Institute of Singles Dynamics found that 43 percent of those responding said their singles group sponsored fundraising projects; 56 percent said they did not. Of those that did, some of the causes their single adult ministries raised money for included: outreach, pro-life, mission trips, overseas missionaries, community service, special speakers, local and regional causes, operational expenses, field trips, church budget, redecorate church hall, supplies, and various ministries.

THE DUAL PURPOSE OF FUNDRAISING

The most obvious purpose for fundraising is to support a worth while cause. Here are a few examples of how several singles groups raised money for charitable causes.

The Saints and Sinners singles group of River Forest, Illinois, raised $11,000 for charity a few years ago. This money was raised by holding dances throughout the year. The money helped support hospitals, schools for handicapped children, and other needy causes in the Chicago area.

The Society for the Arts singles group in Phoenix, Arizona, raised more than $145,000 over the years for various arts groups in their area. Their main method of raising funds is through singles dances.

As we noted in Service Projects, the Village Singles group of Prairie Village, Kansas, annually collects and donates thousands of items and thousands of dollars to many different charities in their area.

But supporting charities, however worthy that may be, is only one reason for singles groups to raise funds. Another important purpose is that it offers opportunities for people to work together and rally behind an altruistic cause. Fundraisers foster a sense of brotherhood.

There are four other tangible benefits to fundraising for your single adult ministry.

1.   It draws people into a project who might not otherwise have found a port of entry to the singles group.
2.   The short-term nature of a fundraising project invites people to volunteer who might not otherwise be able to serve in a long-term capacity, as an officer or committee chair.
3.   It allows other people in the church or community to affirm the single adult ministry by donating to the fundraiser.
4.   It gives volunteers a chance to participate in a common task and create memories they can share for years to come.

UNUSUAL FUNDRAISERS

Here are a few examples of some unusual fundraisers for single adult ministries.

Dining for Dollars

Dining for Dollars is a variation of the Dinners for Eight concept. Single adults in Seattle, Washington, offered to prepare and serve a sumptuous five-course dinner for the first eight people to donate $25 to $100 for a particular cause during the month. Each donor received an invitation with all the specifics—time, location, and appropriate dress. It is a fun and festive way to raise money for a worthy cause and enjoy a fine meal at the same time.

Dollars for Desserts

Dollars for Desserts is a typical bake sale which caters to the working person's desire for home baked goods. Books like Baking for Pleasure and Profit tell you how to target your customer, select the most lucrative locations, and choose the slickest selling times of the day to reach eager customers.[1] For example, a quick munchie or single cookie sells well in a bank parking lot. Or sell baked goods to the church, but the profits will be smaller because of the limited market.

Singles Dance for Jerry's Kids

The Tulsa Singles Council once sponsored a singles dance with all the profits going to Jerry Lewis's Muscular Dystrophy Telethon. You could do something similar to raise support for any charitable organization.

Profits From Pizza

The single adult group can earn extra money by selling and making pizzas. Some pizza establishments allow groups to take advance orders for pizzas then have their members assemble the pizzas at the church. The pizza company provides all the ingredients and supervises the assembly. Pizza companies that offer this service also give pointers on how to publicize this as a fundraising event.

White Elephant Auction

The Colonial Presbyterian singles group in Kansas City sponsored a White Elephant Auction and donated the proceeds to help with the dental expenses of a little boy in Mexico. Invite people to wrap items for auction and not reveal the contents to anyone. This "blind bidding" offers a lot of fun and excitement.

A variation is not to wrap the items and allow people to view what they are bidding on. If several people really want something, the bidding often goes quite high and brings in a lot of money for your cause. Remember, "One man's trash is another man's treasure." Still yet another variation is to offer an auction church wide and invite everyone to bring donated items to the auction. Employ a professional auctioneer—he will be worth his weight in gold and may even donate his time for the cause.

Bidding for Bachelors

Bidding for Bachelors is a fairly new type of charity fundraiser sweeping the country. According to some reports, these auctions are bring tens of thousands of dollars for such causes as the American Cancer Society and multiple sclerosis.

Invite celebrity bachelors to go on a date with whoever wins the bid. Nail down the details well in advance. The bidding can go quite high. At one auction, two women bid a lot of money on a date with a millionaire bachelor who promised to take the winner for an elephant ride while Tiny Tim serenaded them. They kept bidding against each other until they reached $12,000! Finally, the master of ceremonies asked the bachelor to take both of them on separate dates, and he agreed. Each woman paid $12,000 for the privilege.

There may be a number of celebrity-status bachelors (radio/television personalities, business owners/executives, sports figures, civic and political figures, educators, etc.) in your area who would be willing to donate some of their time for such a fun and worthy cause.

The "Thons"

There are many kinds of "thons" a group can do to raise money. They range from a walk-a-thon to tennis-thons. Brainstorm and create your own kind of "thon."

The Silent Auction

I recently noticed a number of organizations having "silent auctions" to raise money for a certain project. My own church recently had one to sell off old equipment and furniture.

People look over the merchandise and determine what they would like to buy. They write down their bid for an item on a piece of paper and turn it in to the appropriate person. All bids are placed into a large envelope and sealed until the appointed time to open them. The items go to the highest bidder.

This could be a fun project for a singles group and a great way to raise money. Most single adults have some unwanted items around their house or apartment that someone else may want. Gather all the items people are willing to donate. Set the deadline for the bids to be turned in. Invite all the singles to participate in opening the bids to see who won what and how much money is raised. Make sure you offer refreshments and allow it to be a social time as well.

A variation is to invite single members to donate their time and expertise to perform various services for other singles (or the entire congregation). Some may donate their time to helping with tax returns, cutting lawns, cleaning house, cooking, doing car repairs, house painting, sewing, or hauling something in their pick-up truck. Those who wish to "buy" these services write down their bids. The bids are opened and the service goes to the top dollar.

Selling Products

There are all kinds of products that can be sold to raise money. Check in your telephone Yellow Pages under "Fundraising Organizations" for a sampling of what's available. Many companies have catalogs full of products to choose from. Discount coupon books are always a popular product to sell.

Don't give up with these ideas. Again, this is just a sampling of suggestions to feed your imagination.

▲

CHAPTER 16

Single-Parent Families

Single-parent families are a special group. This chapter addresses the unique problems of single-parent families. We will conclude with a number of suggestions for churches helping these families.

THE CHILDREN

Single-parent homes are growing fast in America. About one quarter of all families in the United States are single-parent families. Between 40 and 50 percent of all children in this country spend part of their youth in a single-parent home. Children from divorced homes are often said to be from "broken homes." Avoid using this phrase in the presence of a child. The term broken is demeaning—the word itself has a negative impact upon children.

Children from single-parent homes need special care because they have special needs. One report says that 88 percent of all children in single-parent households live with their mothers.[1] And more than half (56 percent) of these children in female-headed households live in poverty.[2] Remember that some of the children of single parents in single adult ministry may be suffering economically.

Many children suffer from paternal deprivation

caused by their father's lack of interest in his children or by their mother's hostility toward her former husband. Of all the children who live with their divorced mothers fewer than half will see their fathers at all during a given year.[3] One national survey found that, over a five-year period, only 10 percent of divorced fathers maintained regular contact with their children—only 5 percent of those children saw their fathers regularly over ten years.[4]

Everyone knows that adults have stress in their lives. But children living in single-parent homes have their own unique set of stresses. According to Lutheran Women magazine, children living in single-parent families may experience some of the following unique stresses in addition to the normal stress of growing up: resentment at change in family lifestyle and finances; resentment at losing a parent; low self-esteem resulting from being treated as different or unacceptable in the neighborhood or church congregation; lack of another adult for support; weariness of resentment and frustration from the custodial parent; feelings of being torn between two families after a divorce; and a sense of personal guilt and responsibility for causing the divorce or death of a parent.[5]

As a result of these stresses, children from single-parent homes have far more than their share of problems coping with school, developing self-esteem, and finding healthy relationships. And sometimes they have trouble with the law.

In a nationwide survey conducted in 1988, researchers for the National Center of Health Statistics found a remarkably high incidence of emotional and academic problems among children living in single-parent families and step families. In addition to the "prevalence of learning disabilities," the findings also revealed "young people from single-parent families or step families were two to three times more likely to have had emotional or behavior problems than those who had both of their biological parents present in the homes."[6]

However, a research team from Johns Hopkins University sity conducted a study of more than 20,000 children which suggests that many of the problems of single-parent children were actually created in sharply dysfunctional families before their parents divorced. This study suggests that divorce itself is not the cause of problems in these children, but rather the severe dysfunction in the marriage while the family was living together.[7]

The wise caregiver knows and understands the dynamics and stresses of children from single-parent homes and realizes that these children need all the love and care they can get. In fact, according to Dr. Lee Salk, "There are ways of dealing with divorce that help children grow in positive ways." Children function better when their divorcing parents "resolve [the divorce]in a sane way, with a minimal display of anger or destructive behavior, and where the wishes and needs of the children are given primary concern."[8]

Again, the wise leader will know these dynamics and offer whatever is available to help these children grow through their parents divorce.

THE PARENTS

Single parents have their own unique set of problems. Single parents have less money and more problems than married couples. Many single parents have to work two jobs to make ends meet. And while they may want to have a quality family life, they simply have less time and energy to spend with their children. This increased stress often has a negative effect on their relationships with their children.[9]

Researcher Judith S. Wallerstein and Sandra Blakeslee support this by saying, "When a marriage breaks down, men and women often become less able to care for their children. They may give less time, provide less discipline, and be less sensitive to their children when they are caught up in the divorce and its aftermath."[10]

But all is not lost. Stories abound of single parents who have had remarkable success in raising their children and maintaining their own careers. Many single parents have discovered that all is not trauma and travail. Single parents often make the best of their financial circumstances despite the fact that the average single parent has far less expendable income than do intact families.

Nevertheless, single parents do have special needs. A survey of 130 single parents in Ohio found that "single parents want information on parenting, self-esteem, handling multiple roles, dealing with children's problems and feelings, and easier ways to maintain a home."[11] Singles leaders must recognize these needs and develop programs to meet those needs.

WHAT CAN THE CHURCH DO?

There is much a sensitive church can do for single-parent families. Here are a few ideas gleaned over the years from various sources and experiences.

- Understand the general dynamics of most single-parent families—more stress, less money, possible resentments, worries about children, etc.
- Do not refer to single-parent homes as "broken homes."
- Provide free child care for every event held at the church.
- Offer scholarships to needy single parents so they can attend programs and events.
- Have a single parents night out on a regular basis

so that parents can have time away from their children to do other things.

- Offer a parenting seminar for single parents.
- Start an after-school program for all children.
- Offer support groups for the kids as well as the parents.
- Purchase books for the church library that deal with single-parent issues.
- Provide counseling and/or make proper referrals to qualified psychological therapists.
- Mobilize helpers when the single parents need help with housework and yard work.
- Don't expect single parents to attend every church committee meeting.
- Create a sense of openness so that the single parents will call when necessary to discuss their needs and problems.
- Establish an "adopt-a-grandchild" program in the church—grandparents share with child care and participate in special times like the children's birthdays and holidays.
- Include positive illustrations of single-parent families in sermons.
- Be aware of the various programs in the community that offer services for single-parent families.
- Encourage a positive relationship with the "other" parent unless it is a clearly destructive relationship.
- Invite single parents and their children to make suggestions about specific ways the single adult ministry can help.

A FINAL WORD

The following quote was taken from an open letter appearing in Parenting Solo: How to Enjoy Life and

Raise Good Kids. This letter is intended as a challenge to all church professionals to be more aware of the needs of single adults and what the church can do to help meet those needs.

Single-parent families do have specialized needs, but at the same time they can become whole just as any family can. Being a church that takes its ministry to families—all families—seriously means more than just providing worship and fellowship experiences. These singles silently cry for support groups, information-sharing times, workshops and ongoing programs designed to meet their real needs. When these things are provided, your church indeed becomes a family church.[12]

AFTERWORD

▲

Several years ago, I received a letter from Jim Arnold, president of the Joint Heirs Singles connected with the People's Church in Fresno,California. I found this quote particularly interesting:

> Starting a singles ministry in your church is a challenge. Think through your principles before you start. A new singles ministry grows by trial and error and step by step. Don't try to hit the top step on your first jump. Ask for help and ideas. If your church has a small singles group, join with other churches.
>
> Many churches avoid singles ministry because of the problems. DON'T GIVE UP. The church of Jesus Christ is here to meet needs and to serve people.
>
> The singles ministry is the most exciting and rewarding thing I have ever done.

Let me echo his sentiment. Single adult ministry is vitally needed and deserves its rightful place in the life of the church. Pray for guidance and God's blessing—and enjoy ministering with single adults. It can be exciting—for the single adults as well as the leaders.

FOR FURTHER READING

The following list of books from Thomas Nelson can help you understand some of the specific needs in your single adult ministry. Resources such as these can provide comfort, understanding, guidance, and spiritual strength for anyone who is single or who counsels and cares for single adults.

The Fresh Start Divorce Recovery Workbook by Bob Burns and Tom Whiteman
The Fresh Start Single Parenting Workbook by Dr. Thomas Whiteman with Randy Peterson
Innocent Victims by Dr. Thomas Whiteman with Randy Peterson
Kids Caught in the Middle by Gary Sprague with Randy Peterson
Single Mothers Raising Sons by Dr. Bobbie Reed
His, Hers, and Theirs by Larry and Shawna Frenzel
When You're Serious About Love by Dr. Kay Kuzma
Becoming a Friend and Lover by Dick Purnell
Too Close, Too Soon by Jim A. Talley and Bobbie Reed
Before the Ring: Questions Worth Asking by William L. Coleman
Getting Ready for Marriage Workbook by Jerry D. Hardin and Dianne C. Sloan

The author also publishes an extensive annotated bibliography that describes more than three hundred books dealing with singles and singles ministry. The bibliography is updated periodically and is available for $6.00 through the Institute of Singles Dynamics, P. O. Box 11394, Kansas City, Missouri 64112. Write for bulk copy rates.

A P P E N D I X

▲

While single adults have some things in common, they are also diverse and don't like to be stereotyped. Nevertheless, here are some key observations and cardinal rules for working with singles. Most of these points have already been made in the book, but they bear repeating. You can use this list as a quick reference.

KEY OBSERVATIONS

1. Expect a lot of "shoppers" to attend your group. That's par for the course.

2. Single adults often wait until the last minute before making definite plans for group social activities.

3. Single persons in transition who attend a church singles group will have more loyalty to the group than to the church itself.

4. Accept the fact that there will be a high turnover of singles who attend your programs.

5. Many single adults want to be active in church. Encourage them to do so.

6. There are more singles in your church than you probably imagine.

7. Single adults are more mobile than marrieds.

8. Anticipate that some of your staunch church

members may believe myths about singles and misunderstand the mission of your group.

9. The process of educating your singles about group conduct and policy will be ongoing.

10. Single adults will support the programs and activities they have helped initiate and plan.

CARDINAL RULES

1. Don't rush new members into key leadership positions.

2. To keep "fresh blood" in leadership, don't let an officer serve two consecutive terms in the same position, unless absolutely necessary.

3. Be a good listener. Everyone has a story to tell.

4. When your singles marry, move them out of the singles group gently but quickly.

5. When choosing teams, do it by numbering off, not by picking sides.

6. Don't assume that a person would be more active if he or she had a job to do.

7. Vary the programs and lessons you offer. People enjoy variety.

8. Watch your terminology. Don't use degrading terms such as pairs and spares, fifth wheel, or broken home.

9. Allow single adults to have social motives when they attend programs.

10. Remember your single members on special occasions such as birthdays.

11. Plan lots of fun, light activities, and place a high value on healthy group humor.

12. To avoid burnout, maintain your own spiritual life.

13. Let a person's payment be a reservation for an activity, not verbal agreement. People often forget commitments, unless they've paid in advance.

14. Leave some things unorganized to invite participation from new people and those without official duties.

15. Don't print a person's home phone number on a group roster if he or she objects.

16. Don't be afraid to say, "I don't know," or "I'm sorry."

17. The singles minister does not have to attend every social event. Single adults are adults; give them some space.

18. Set an example of promptness, preparedness, politeness, and piety.

19. Don't try to do it all. Delegate whatever you can.

20. Always provide child care for singles programs and activities held on church property.

N O T E S

Introduction

1. For subscription rates, write to: Single Adult Unit, Family Ministries Department, 127 9th Ave. North, Nashville, TN 37234.

Chapter 1

1. Current Population Survey, "Marital Status and Living Arrangements," table 1, U.S. Bureau of the Census, March 1991, p. 15.
2. Lyle Schaller, "You and Your Unchurched Neighbor," Lutheran Standard, Jan. 1985, p. 4-7.

Chapter 2

1. "How Much Do You Know About Being Single?" Kansas City Times, 1 Dec. 1977, p. A-14.
2. Jeanne S. Hurlbut and Alan A. Acock, "The Effects of Marital Status on the Form and Composition of Social Networks," Social Science Quarterly 71 (1990), pp. 163-173.
3. "Multi-Church Affiliations," Ministry Currents, April 1990, p. 6.
4. Nicholas Zill and Charlotte Schoenborn, "Developmental, Learning and Emotional Problems: Health of Our Nation's Children, United States, 1988," Vital and Health Statistics of the National Center for Health Statistics, Bureau of the Census, 16 Nov. 1990, pp. 8-
5. Jeffrey Young, Ph.D., "Loneliness," U.S. News & World Report, 17 Sept. 1987.
6. Randy Page and Galen Cole, "Demographic Predictors of Self-Reported Loneliness in Adults," Psychological Reports 68 (1991), pp. 939-945.
7. K. R. Petronis, et al., "An Epidemiologic Investigation of Potential Risk Factors in Suicide Attempts," Social Psychiatry and Psychiatric Epidemiology 35 (1990).
8. Susan Kennedy, et al., "Immunological Consequences of Acute and Chronic Stressors," British Journal of Medical Psychology 61 (1988), pp. 77-85.
9. Jeffrey Young, Ph.D., "Loneliness," U.S. News & World Report, 17 Sept. 1987.
10. George Gallup, Jr., and Jim Castelli, "Marriage bolsters in-

terest in religion," Kansas City Times, 5 March 1988, p. E-10.

11. "Churched and Unchurched Singles," Single Adults in America, 1987, p. 17.

Chapter 3

1. Paul G. Friedman, ed., "Work Wonders Express Thanks," The Pryor Report (Clemson, SC: Fred Pryor Resources), taken from Sheila M. Bethel, Making a Difference: Twelve Qualities That Make You a Leader (New York: Putnam, 1990), Oct. 1990.

2. Dick Tibbits, "When Should You Refer?" Ministry Magazine, May 1987, p. 20.

Chapter 5

1. Dianne Swaim, "A Functioning Single Adult Council," The Christian Single, July 1991.

Chapter 6

1. Tim Unsworth, ed., "Getting Out Is Going Up," U.S. Parish, Jan. 1991, p. 4.

Chapter 7

1. Church Ad Project, 1021 Diffley Rd., Eagan, MN 55123. Phone: 1-800-331-9391.

2. The author offers a kit on singles seminars through community colleges. For a kit, send $5.00 to Don Davidson, P.O. Box 11394, Kansas City, MO 64112.

Chapter 10

1. Bill Sullivan, "Incorporation: Welcoming Newcomers," Small Group Newsletter (Colorado Springs, CO: The Navigators), April 1986.

2. Win Arn, "Can We Close the Back Door," Pastoral Newsletter (Ann Arbor, MI: The Center for Pastoral Renewal), Feb. 1986.

Chapter 12

1. Robert Barber, "A Christian Approach to Divorce Support Groups," The Christian Ministry, Jan./Feb. 1989. Reprinted by permission of Christian Ministry Foundation.

Chapter 13

1. Single Adults in America (Glendale, CA: Barna Research Group, 1987), p. 26.

Chapter 15

1. Baking for Pleasure and Profit (Woodridge, IL: Wilton Enterprises, Inc., 1982).

Chapter 16

1. "Statistical Abstract," note 35, table 69, U.S. Bureau of the Census.
2. Terry Arendell, Mothers and Divorce (Berkeley: University of California Press, 1986), note 23, table 6, p. 173.
3. Leonore Weitzman, The Divorce Revolution (New York: The Free Press, 1985), note 2, p. 369.
4. Frank F. Furstenberg, Jr., and Kathleen M. Harris, "The Disappearing American Father," unpublished paper, University of Pennsylvania, March 1990.
5. Terry Schultz, ed., Lutheran Women (Philadelphia: Lutheran Church in America, date unknown).
6. Nicholas Zill and Charlotte Schoenborn, "Developmental, Learning and Emotional Problems: Health of Our Nation's Children, United States, 1988," Vital and Health Statistics of the National Center for Health Statistics, 16 Nov. 1990, pp. 8-9.
7. Andrew J. Cherlin, "Soured marriages, not divorces, hurt children more, study says," Kansas City Star, 7 June 1991, p. A-5.
8. Lee Salk, as quoted in "Divorce Doesn't Have to Shatter Children," Kansas City Star, 14 May 1991, p. E-3.
9. Ronald L. Mullis, "Reports of Child Behavior by Single Mothers and Married Mothers," Child Study Journal no. 17 (1987), pp. 211-225.
10. Judith S. Wallerstein and Sandra Blakeslee, Second Chances (New York: Ticknow & Fields, 1989).
11. Janet Jacobson, "Singles News Briefs," Arizona Solo, June 1988.
12. Emil J. Authelet, Parenting Solo: How to Enjoy Life and Raise Good Kids (San Bernardino, CA: Here's Life Publishers, 1989), p. 226.

About the Author

Don Davidson is a single-again, Kansas City pastor who has started several successful singles groups, served as a consultant with numerous churches, presented hundreds of seminars, and developed a variety of resources for other singles leaders nationwide. He is also the director of the Institute of Singles Dynamics based in Kansas City. This nonprofit organization conducts leadership seminars on singles ministry and publishes SAMI (Single Adult Ministry Information), America's first national newsletter for singles leaders.

Davidson is a native Tulsan and a graduate of the University of Tulsa and Midwestern Baptist Theological Seminary. He is in demand as a seminar speaker and consultant to churches, businesses, and community colleges interested in reaching the singles market with their programs and services. He has two adult sons, David and Andrew.

If you are interested in more information about the Institute of Singles Dynamics, please write to Don Davidson, Institute of Singles Dynamics, P.O. Box 11394, Kansas City, Missouri 64112.